GREAT PERFORMANCES

Clemens Rettich

GREAT PERFORMANCES

The Small Business Script for the 21st Century

Clemens Rettich

For Sheila

Who showed me how the big picture and
the fine details work together

Acknowledgements

Great Performances was launched pretty much the way most small businesses are launched: I had an idea, started to make it real, and then met someone who showed me I really didn't have a clue what I was doing! I was shown just how dangerously little I knew, and then provided with the most amazing tools to get the job done by Julie Salisbury of Influence Publishing. I am confident in the usefulness of the content, but if I have had any success at all in shaping all of that into an honest book, that credit goes to Julie.

The single most important element of any great performance is relentless daily effort. My guide, muse, and support is my wife Sheila. Plain and simple this book could not have been written at all without her support and wisdom. Talking with Sheila lead to new ideas, to bad ideas thankfully discarded, and to great ideas promoted when I wasn't sure of them. This book is a result of her support and ongoing insistence I do what it takes to get this finished. If this book becomes any reflection at all of what Sheila has invested in me and in this book, then it is going to do just fine!

Thanks also go to Todd Humen B.Sc. C.A. for his review of a couple of the key sections dealing with money. Precision of language is always important in business, but nowhere more so than when dealing with finances.

As a group I also have to thank the men and women in the world of small business and small business support who have been a constant source of support or inspiration or both: Brent Boyd, Seth Godin, Jeff Hilton, John Jantsch, Darlene Munn, Terry O'Reilly, Cathy Robertson, David Rendall, Scott Ritter, Bret

Simmons, Cheryl Thomas, Steve Yastrow, Michael Watkins, and Taffy Williams.

Maeve Maguire provided copy editing services and saved me from some embarrassing and misguided entries. In carefully going through Maeve's edit I also learned I have some distracting tics as a writer I have since been working on. Just like working with Julie, working with Maeve as a writing professional has been a decision I am happy I made. Getting the support of professionals: priceless.

Two final groups must be appreciated in their contribution to both this book and to where I am in my life now. All of the clients who have trusted me with the growth of their businesses, the security of their families, and the vitality of their dreams, are the true inspiration and motivation of this work. Their blood, sweat, and tears keep me focused. Their search for that Great Performance has been the force driving me to get this book out and into their hands. I can honestly say I get out of bed every morning excited to play a role in the success of my clients. If this book plays even a small part in doing that for the community of all small business owners out there, I will have succeeded where it matters.

To all of the artists, musicians, dancers, and actors who have inspired and taught me over the years, my thanks. I want in that same space to thank my parents Konrad and Ursula who have taught me to love the arts and the unique lessons they teach us about the interplay of work, discipline, creativity, and success. Great composers, dancers, players, and actors are a constant reminder creativity and discipline are not mutually exclusive, and the best way to achieve that Great Performance is to do something again and again. And again. What is great is seldom easy, and the greatest joy is in finally getting the truly challenging right. That is the lesson all of the arts and artists have taught me, and I seek to share with all small businesses owners as they strive for their own Great Performances.

Contents

Dedication
Acknowledgements
Contents

Prelude

No young person who ever dreamed of playing guitar picked one up for the first time and said to herself, "I am going to be awesome at this."

What she did do is pick up that guitar like she was picking up an artifact from a dream, and think to herself, "I am going to awesome at this." The instrument in her hands was from a future where she was going to be amazing, a star. When she closed her eyes, all she could see is one great performance after another, screaming fans and all.

If your dream of starting a business shares or shared that expectation of a Great Performance, then this book is for you.

This Is A Great Performance

For our purposes, a Great Performance in business looks like this:
- Creating something you have dreamed of;
- Working in something you love;
- Providing a life for yourself and your family – with time and money to live fully;
- An exit that leaves you enriched and independent.

This book is not about best practices.
Best practices assume that what works for business A works for business B. In the 21st century, where we are moving from a world

1

based on repeatable, mass-produced commodities, to a world of relationships and social webs, a world of the "'many unique'": what works for one business simply cannot be reproduced successfully to work in another business.

Neither is this a blue-sky you-can-do-anything-you-want book of inspiration.

This is a book of the principles, ideas, and actions that will create a great small business performance in the 21st century.

Great Performances brings together ideas and actions I have collected from working beside small-business owners in pursuit of their dreams. As I have experienced them, the items in this book are the things that have made a difference; sometimes they have been the difference between a great performance and failure.

Sadly, many of the items in this book find themselves here not because I saw them done well; they are here because they are as absent from many small businesses as they are important. Far too often I have conducted my initial assessment of a business only to find the absence of one of these items crippling the business.

♫

Business Is An Art

I started my professional life many years ago as a classical musician. As the years and my restless interests moved me ever more deeply into the world of business, I carried that training as a musician with me. It is that training and perspective that I bring to this book.

Great Performances in the performing arts have not only shaped some of the languages and images here, but they have informed a basic belief: nothing great is accomplished without knowing the fundamentals and practicing them. When ambitious vision and disciplined practice come together, truly amazing things happen.

That mix is what I want to bring to you in this book: an inspiring vision of what truly great business looks like, and a generous helping of useful tips, guides, and practice techniques designed to help you achieve that vision.

A creative vision also shapes the structure of this book. Divided into Acts, Scenes, and Intermissions, the sections themselves are as much song, poem, and story as step-by-step how-to lists. This book is shaped by the stories, Great Performances - and tragic disasters - of the business and business owners I have worked with over the years.

Some themes are central to every Great Performance, and I have woven them through this book: the importance of people; the importance of consistent systems; the importance of great visions and great leadership; the importance of dealing with the tiniest detail of your business with the focus of a classical violinist.

Each of the three main sections of the book is called an Act for two reasons: it contains and continues the idea of a performance, and it focuses on the idea of acting. There are a million great business ideas out there. Not only are there many, but they have also been around in some cases for hundreds of years. What makes an idea a good one is when it is used well and consistently to great results.

Sooner or later, you have to act.

In brief, here are the three Acts of the book:

Act I – Putting People First

In Act I we focus on the values and actions of putting people first. We focus first on customers, then on employees. For a Great Performance in this 'social century', focusing on people and relationships first is an absolute precondition for success.

3

Act II - Maximizing Limited Resources

Infinite growth, the gospel of the industrial-age business model, depends on infinite resources. If there is one thing we have learned (or at least anyone who is paying attention has), it is that we do not have unlimited resources on this earth.

This Act explores the three resources every business shares: people, time, and money. I look at the possibilities and limitations of each resource, and explore the possibilities for getting the most out of each one.

Act III - Planning Your Exit

There is no possible way of introducing this Act without quoting Stephen Covey: "Begin with the end in mind."

One of the most predictable causes for the long-term failure of a small business is the absence of an exit strategy. Most small-business owners have no idea what one is, or assume that it is just for other folks, like wealthy serial entrepreneurs building their 4th high-tech startup. Nothing could be further from the truth.

Every small business owner must have a vision, and eventually a clear plan, for how their relationship with their business will end. The failure to have this in place means that all you will have is a few decades of self-employment, with no pension or any other means of supporting yourself when you can no longer work in the business.

The final Act explores why it is important to have an exit strategy, what some of the options are, and suggests actions you can take to ensure that your Great Performance ends in a standing ovation!

♫

What You Need First

I can, of course, make no guarantees. No one can promise you that your business will be the outrageous success you dream it will be.

In our case, you will need 3 preconditions for success in place before anything in this book will be of value to your business. Without them, the whole enterprise is a nonstarter.

If you do have the following three fundamentals in place, and do everything else that I have laid out in this book, you will have everything in place for a Great Performance.

Here are the 3 preconditions for success:

1. There is a market for what you have to offer, and you have access to that market.
2. You have the resources (time, people, and money) to leverage the growth of your business for at least 3 to 5 years of very hard times.
3. You have some business training, or access to a mentor or coach who can guide you through the complex basics of running a business.

With the 3 fundamentals in place and a commitment to use the 15 Scenes in this book to shape your daily decisions, only a natural disaster or forces beyond anyone's control should derail you from achieving a Great Performance in your business.

♫

Is This For Everyone?

Along with the three preconditions for success laid out above, there is one more thing worth reflecting on before proceeding:

Who are you? Do you have what it takes to run and grow a small business?

It's not about brains or education or money. It is about being comfortable leading.

The strengths of a successful business owner include visioning, planning, risk-taking, communicating, motivating: being a leader in the fullest sense. You have to be the kind of person for whom those activities and approaches to life are a comfortable fit.

I have met bright, competent people who struggled every day with the business they were trying to grow. They had everything in place except for those leadership qualities. They were not fundamentally optimistic, they were not comfortable with higher levels of risk, they struggled to find the right mix of leading, motivating, and micromanaging.

These people would make great employees, amazing managers, and even wonderful business partners, but as my mother loves to say, *"Man kann einfach nicht über seinen eigenen Schatten springen."* Literally translated that means, "One can simply not jump over one's own shadow." You cannot be other than who you are.

Owning and growing a small business successfully is one of the hardest things anyone could do. Know who you are, and spend some time talking to mentors and coaches in the field to decide if this really is a good fit for you.

If you decide you are that person, and this life is for you, then please dive into this book. One day, please share the story of your Great Performance with me.

♫♫♫

The Program

This book is divided into 3 Acts: People, Resources, and Exits. Each Act contains a number of short essays I have called Scenes. Each Act begins with a pair of case stories: the Band Camp Case

Story tells of a business that is struggling and exposes some of the reasons why; the Great Performance Case Story reveals the story of a business that is doing everything right in the context of the topics covered in that Act.

The names and businesses in the case stories are fictionalized, but each one is based on a real business or composite of two or three real businesses I have encountered. In some cases my relationship with them went no further than an initial assessment, and in others they became clients for years. Some are still clients.

Each Scene begins with a summary statement of what constitutes a Band Camp Performance and a Great Performance in business as it relates to the content of that essay.

Nothing Wrong With Band Camp

Let me make one small note before continuing: I have nothing against band camps!

I use the term "Band Camp" throughout the book as a playful juxtaposition to a Great Performance. Almost every great musician in recent history either attended some form of band camp, or its rock-and-roll equivalent, the garage band.

Everyone starts somewhere, so no disrespect intended. The language is just an acknowledgement that in business and in the vision of a lifetime, remaining in Band Camp is not what we dream.

♫

Places To Pause

Each Scene is punctuated with a Journal Intermission. I suggest reading through this book with a notebook and pen beside you. The journal intermissions are an opportunity to stop, take a breath, and reflect on what you have read by responding to the questions.

You will also find the notation *Flash Point* a few times in the book. These are points I believe must be tended to by a business owner if they haven't already done so. Typically there can be serious business, legal, or financial risks to not attending to these items.

Each act ends with Master Classes. These are checklists of concrete action steps your business must undertake to achieve a Great Performance.

While the Master Class lists are intended to be taken on in sequence, there are some items that are labeled *Do It Now*, meaning if this is something you are not doing in your business, forget the sequence and get this addressed right now!

With those program notes to explain how this all works, let's get started!

♫♫♫

ACT I:
PUTTING PEOPLE FIRST

Performance Note
"People who matter are most aware
that everyone else does, too."
Malcolm S. Forbes

THE CASE STORIES

Band Camp Performance

Campbell's Pharmacy had been in the family for 3 generations. Rod Campbell was the third-generation pharmacist and owner of the business for 12 years. The business had a good profile in the local community, and was seen as an established part of the retail landscape.

Revenues were stable and staff turnover was not unreasonable. So why was Campbell's Pharmacy losing more money with each passing month? That was the question on the table when I was brought in to have a look around.

At first glance, and through the initial formal assessment, nothing unusual turned up. It was only on a deeper look, and after spending time interviewing staff and reviewing daily procedures, what was wrong started to add up.

At first the issues seemed unrelated: inventory was unmanaged;

customer retention and repeat business was low; a lot of the staff had been in the same position for years without any advancement and had no interest in training or incentive programs; and dollars-per-transaction were low for the industry.

Rod agreed that some things could be improved, but couldn't understand his staff's reluctance to get on board with training, incentives, or anything that improved the situation for themselves, their customers, or Campbell's Pharmacy. Some of the staff had been there for years. This looked like low turnover, high loyalty, and generally a good thing. The truth was far different.

It finally came together when I interviewed the staff individually. A disturbing picture emerged.

Here is what was really going on:

- The senior staff had been there for years but their performance did not match their seniority or pay. Early on Rod had been afraid to lose staff and so paid too much too soon. They were still paid well, but he could not afford to give them any more raises.
- There was no faith in any training or sales initiatives Rod brought in. Staff said nothing ever worked and they didn't see why they should make the effort when every new program was a flavour of the month, quickly to be replaced by another scheme to save the business.
- The whole organization was infected with gossip and backbiting. Junior staff in particular resented what they saw as favouritism and inconsistencies when it came to expectations. They saw that senior staff did nothing to earn their positions and weren't held accountable for any kind of performance.
- Bullied by his staff and by his suppliers, Rod ordered far too much inventory. Poor inventory control, steep discounting, and poor sales and service skills on the part of staff meant that profit margins ranged between thin and nonexistent.

The consequences for business were clear: inventory was ordered on a whim and with the hope it would sell; staff refused to improve their sales and customer service skills; customers only came into the pharmacy out of convenience or habit or because of steep discounts; staff were hard to find and generally unpleasant to talk to; Campbell's Pharmacy struggled to pay its suppliers on time; the line of credit was maxed out; and the owner was paying himself less and less with each passing month.

At this rate, Campbell's Pharmacy would be out of business in 18 months, after being in the community for 3 generations.

♬

Great Performance

Marina knew it was a great job before she even landed it.

She applied to a hair salon to work as an assistant. The first interview was with the owner and lasted ten minutes. The owner had asked Marina a few questions that seemed to have nothing to do with work or hair; just conversation about friends and family.

That evening, the salon manager phoned her and told her that her references had checked out nicely, and asked if she could come in for a half day to meet the rest of the staff and check out the salon.

During that second visit, the manager gave her a tour and introduced her to some of the other employees. At one point the manager said she had to get back to work and left Marina to have a cup of coffee with a stylist who was on a break. The stylist seemed very excited to meet someone new and asked Marina lots of questions about what she thought of the salon, the manager, the neighborhood, and so on.

At one point Marina had a chance to try her hand at a shampoo, as a couple of newer assistants were practicing shampoos and scalp massages on each other.

The whole time the questions and the social chatter never stopped.

Marina loved the openness. She felt she was able to ask anything, and everyone obviously loved working at the salon regardless of their roles or how long they had been there. The place was spotless, and everyone was constantly moving. The energy was positive and infectious, with employees being visibly supportive of each other.

Marina was thrilled when she was offered the job, even though the offer came with the warning to not consider the job was hers until the 90-day probationary period was over. The manager told her she should consider the next three months just an extended interview.

The three months were hard work, but Marina quickly saw why the salon was so successful and everyone was so positive.

The way things were done in the salon was very structured. Almost everything had a right way to do it and Marina spent the first couple of weeks reading the Salon Handbook, absorbing as many of the details as she could. Everything from employee clothing and makeup, to how guests were addressed, how they were moved from reception to hair or shampoo stations and back again, to how things were displayed, cleaned, and sold. Just about everything seemed to have a 'right way' of doing it.

There were lots of meetings, training sessions, formal education, and different kinds of games and role play, each of which Marina quickly learned had a purpose. Despite the high level of structure, employees had a lot of decisions they had to make on their own, and expectations were clearly high to 'figure it out' when something didn't fit standard procedure.

Marina often felt just outside of her comfort zone. It was hard work, but three things got Marina out of bed every morning ready for more:

1. The salon was clearly successful. The phone never stopped ringing. The senior stylists had 18-month waiting lists and

drove really nice cars. The owner of this salon owned two other salons that were apparently run exactly the same way, and were just as successful. The salon managers were accomplished professionals who clearly loved their jobs and had the respect of everyone including the owner.

2. Everyone did what it took to make things work. Marina had never seen anyone shirk a responsibility because it wasn't their job. Marina could see how hard the managers worked to mix in each new employee like a colour in a great painting, or an ingredient in a memorable meal. The result was a team where everyone used personal initiative to push the success of the team higher and higher.

3. Marina received constant feedback and support. For the first year or so, she did pretty much everything from sweeping to shampooing to posting information on the salon's Facebook page. In that year, the salon manager had discovered that Marina was a born organizer.

Every time Marina came in for her shift, the first thing she would do, without even thinking about it, was turn every bottle of product on the shelves to face the same way. The manager repeatedly told her how much that attention to order and appearance was appreciated, and gave her every opportunity to do more.

By the end of her third year, Marina was in charge of inventory and salon displays. She would come in on holidays and weekends to stay on top of inventory and make sure the salon always wowed people when they walked through the doors, yet she never resented a moment of the extra work. Marina heard over and over again how much her attention to detail and her little touches added to the experience of the salon and supported the rest of the team. The owner took her to a trade show in Las Vegas where she learned more in one week about retail than she thought she could in a year.

At the end of her fourth year, Marina was offered a position as assistant retail manager for all three salons. She was told the pay increase would be modest (though she was already making more money than she thought she would by this point), the hours would go through the roof, and she would have a lot more responsibility.

Marina didn't wait one loud heartbeat before accepting the position. She knew this would be the start of another amazing set of years.

I had coached the owner of this salon for two years at this point, and was asked for feedback on Marina's proposed promotion. I had the same reaction Marina did: this was just the start of something truly amazing.

♪♪♪

Scene 1: Where It All Starts: Customer Relationships

Performance Note
*"Profit in business comes from repeat customers,
customers that boast about your project or service,
and that bring friends with them."*
W. Edwards Deming

Band Camp Performance:

Focusing entirely on promotion and acquiring new business; using a 'see what sticks' approach to marketing; treating every customer the same.

Great Performance:

Managing the entire cycle of a customer's relationship; integrating your brand, your culture, and your vision for a great customer experience.

♫

Stripped to its bare essence, business is one thing: one human being meeting the needs or desires of another human, in exchange for some benefit. We all have needs and desires, but we do not all have the ability to fulfill them for ourselves. We are not all farmers or electricians or mechanics. This is where our fellow humans come in.

♫

There is a memorable scene in 1972s The Godfather:

> Tom (Robert Duvall): *"Your father wouldn't want to hear this, Sonny. This is business not personal."*
> Sonny (James Caan): *"They shoot my father and it's business, my ass!"*
> Tom: *"Even shooting your father was business not personal, Sonny!"*

That phrase "It's business, not personal" has been repeated a million times since then. But for all that it has never been true. Even in the film, as Tom says it, it is meant to be ironic. Everything that Sonny and Michael (Al Pacino) do in the Godfather is personal. Of course it's personal; it's always personal!

A customer's needs, ranging from the basics of food and shelter, to belonging and feeling like we matter, are all very personal.

There was a time when, post-Industrial Revolution, the age of relentless automation worked very hard to turn every need and desire fulfillment into an automated transaction, into a commodity; something that could be repeated perfectly, mechanically, and endlessly.

In the last quarter of the 20th century, that began to turn. The rise of the internet, and the fact we were drowning ourselves in stuff, brought the relationship, the personal, the unique, and the idiosyncratic back into the world of business. Individuality, craft, experience, and relationship are slowly eclipsing the old world of the assembly line and the vending machine.

Not that assembly lines or cheap goods are going anywhere soon. The relentless competitive pressures on pricing will ensure that cheap manufacturing will continue to be a backbone of many businesses and even whole economies for the foreseeable future. It just isn't enough to guarantee success any more. As consumers and employees, we are demanding more.

Small businesses that want to create a Great Performance must be able to deliver that more. It starts with people. People, not markets or human resources. Just people.

A discussion of the role of people in a business could start from one of two places: employees or customers.

While I believe that employees and the culture you build with them are the most critical success factor in the long-term health of a business, the truth is many business owners reading this book don't have employees yet! So we will start with customers.

While you need great employees and a great team culture to achieve a Great Performance over the long haul, you won't get anywhere at all without customers.

So... how many customers do you need to start a business?

Answer: one.

You only need one customer to start a business.

IF...

If you can get one customer, and if you can deliver a remarkable experience that gets her to talk about your business to her friends and family, and if you can confirm the experience of that first customer by providing consistently remarkable experiences to all of her friends and family, you will have taken the single most important step in creating a Great Performance for your business.

You will also understand why I spend almost no time in Act I on acquiring customers (advertising and promotion) and almost every word on retaining customers (customer retention).

After all, how hard can it be to get one customer?

♫

The Cult Of The New

The relationships you have with your existing customers are the most valuable asset you have. Nurturing that must always be a priority over acquiring new customers.

So why do businesses focus so much on customer acquisition when so much evidence and common sense points to the fact this is not the best strategy? I think it has a lot to do with a deeply consumer- and commodity-oriented mindset we have developed in North America over the last century.

"Out with the old and in with the new" has been the rallying cry of a consumer-driven economy for decades now. Hanging onto what you already have just isn't done any more.

Since the end of the Second World War, the sense of endlessly expanding markets, and an unending supply of new commodities to feed them, has permeated our culture. We treat customers like we treat fashions: there will always be a new one next season. Everything (including people) is a disposable commodity. It wasn't always that way.

A few centuries ago, and still in many small communities, there was only repeat business. People bought their goods from the same businesses and families for generations. The millers, builders, bakers, lawyers your parents did business with, were probably the same ones you would do business with. A business that treated you badly would not see your family's trade again for generations.

With mass production, we broke that model and introduced one based entirely on growth, change, and consumption. Hanging onto old friends just wasn't in vogue any more. New became the most important word in the business lexicon.

While those markets changed, and are now changing back again, the economics of retention versus acquisition haven't. A satisfied customer who walks back through your door has cost you little to nothing. Every new customer (unless they are a word-of-mouth referral from that satisfied customer), represent a portion of an advertising budget.

Happy returning customers refer others, and a referred customer is also more profitable than one acquired through advertising. Depending on the business, it can be up to 700% more profitable to retain than to acquire new customers.

The Customer Experience Spiral

Performance Note
A Great Performance requires you manage a customer's experience even after the cash register rings.

To coax a Great Performance out of your customer relationships, you have to see that relationship as extending far beyond the moment of sale. A relationship that only lasts as long as the moment of sale is no relationship at all.

You must manage a customer's experience of your business as a spiraling narrative: it starts from the moment they first hear about your business, through the decision to come in and see you, through the whole purchase process, and into the follow-through you do for the days, weeks, or months after they have walked happily out into the sunshine, purchase in hand. It includes key elements like rewarding customers for their loyalty, and maximizing opportunities to show what you are made of if something goes wrong.

I see it as a spiral because, unlike a circle, the next iteration is not exactly the same; it should be slightly better, slightly higher. It should continue to improve each time they experience that story for themselves.

Remember that consistency itself is a factor in positive customer experiences. You don't need to add new bells and whistles to every visit. One Great Performance is fantastic. Repeat Great Performances when they bring their friends along and everything is as good as they said it would be, that is remarkable - and remarkable is the fuel for great customer experience spirals.

Let's look at ways to build those happy, returning, and referring customer relationships.

Use Lists

One of the questions I ask when I start working with a client is if the business has a customer relationship management (CRM) system. That doesn't mean I am looking for a complex or expensive CRM software package. It just means that I want to know if the business is handling customer relationships in a systematic way. If you don't have a fancy point of sale system or CRM software, a basic spreadsheet or database will do. Anything that lets you record your customers' contact information, preferences, and some quantifiable value they bring to the business, is worth getting started on.

There is no excuse for not having a living, breathing, constantly updated customer list. No Great Performance is possible without it.

Create An A-List

Not all fans and not all relationships with your business are created equal. You must know who your top customers are, based on revenues and referrals. It is poor management of your marketing resources to acknowledge or reward every customer equally. Sort your customers by revenues and referrals. Your A-list is your top revenue sources, AA are top referrers, and Triple-A is that small handful of customers (there won't be many) who are both top referrers and your best paying customers.

Meet Pareto

Knowing which customers are more likely to yield a return on your investment is very important. This is a practical application of the rule known as the *Pareto principle*, also known (incorrectly) as the 80/20 rule.

Any time when the *smaller* number of something is responsible for *greater value* some effect, that is called a Pareto distribution.

For example if 28% of your customers are responsible for 69% of your revenues, you have a Pareto distribution. In its most popular form it is called the 80/20 Rule because there are many examples of 20% of some population, community, or workforce being responsible for 80% of some behaviour.

The person after whom the distribution is named, Vilfredo Pareto, documented in the early twentieth century that 20% of the Italian population owned 80% of the Italian landmass.

In business, it is commonly stated that 20% of your customers *are* responsible for 80% of your revenues. While this is not always literally true, it is generally true that a minority of your customers are responsible for a majority of your business - and that number cannot be easily changed or changed at all. You will never turn that equation on its head by somehow getting the majority of your customers to change their behaviour.

This is why it is so important to make getting to know your A-List customers such a key part of your Great Performance. You will never get the best return on your marketing and retention dollars by spending them equally on all of your customers. Success lies in focusing your heart and your resources on that minority that has done the same for you! Focus your attentions on customers who have already focused their attentions on you.

My Friend Sue Sent Me

Referred business is more profitable and more loyal than business that arrives as the result of direct promotions.

To reward your referrers and to know the value of their referrals, you have to track referrals. There are dozens of ways to do this. Dedicated CRM software can be a big help. You can also provide incentives using print pieces like cards stating the name of the referring customer, and who they referred. You can develop online referral programs that harvest names and email addresses—and you can just ask.

The value in this tracking lies in your ability to identify, nurture, and reward, those customers who are key referral centers. You can't say, "Thank you for that referral" if you don't know who to thank. Any opportunity missed to say thank you is an opportunity missed to grow your business.

Connect. Remarkably.

One of my clients goes through his A-list customers every week and randomly selects someone to deliver a bouquet of flowers to. The card thanks the recipient for being a remarkable customer, and lets them know they are appreciated.

Do you think a random gift like that is going to generate positive word-of-mouth? Absolutely!

One of the keys to creating a Great Performance in musical theatre is to write a tune that lingers in the mind long after the show has wrapped. In the referral business, positive and remarkable stories about your business are that tune.

Performance Note
Follow-through is the rocket fuel of a
great customer retention performance.

Follow-Through

All of your customers, not just your A-list, should receive some form of communication from you after the purchase. A card, a gift certificate, an email newsletter, a phone call... something!

So many businesses say they care more about us than just our money or the sale. Then how come we never hear from them after that sale? Actions speak louder than words, and in the cynical, jaded, and amped-experience world we live in, if you don't walk your walk, and walk it remarkably and consistently, you may as well not exist.

We'll go into much greater detail on the value and how-to of follow-through in the next scene.

Add Value Through Follow-up

In a workshop I once had the owner of a very fine toy shop tell me she couldn't imagine what communication her customers could be interested in. My response? *"How about childhood development, gender issues, toy safety, Christmas trends, fine motor skill development, unusual toys…?"*

Give me a business and in 5 minutes I can come up with a couple of dozen topics its customers might want to know more about. Most businesses have access to information their customers care about.

A newsletter (email or physical) that continues to add value to customers' lives in your area of expertise is a very effective way to stay front of mind. That effectiveness is further amplified if you minimize or eliminate any direct sales messages.

Somehow, somewhere, find a way to stay connected. Continue to provide value. The customer experience spiral I described earlier is driven by follow through.

Develop Tools And Training

You as the business owner cannot be the one (or at least not the only one) managing customer experience and relationships. You have to train your staff in the value of acknowledging and creating repeat business. This means training in both the why and the how. If a customer comes back, it will probably be because of how your staff treated them.

Give your staff the tools to record customer contact information, buying habits, and preferences. Even if it is just a little notebook at the till—that's a start. If you can use more formal systems, like point-of-sale (POS) or customer relationship management (CRM) software, all the better—but do something.

It's Personal. Again.

Your team must understand why customer relationships matter, exactly how to develop those relationships, and be encouraged to build real relationships using their own strengths and personalities.

Make it clear that the section on CRM in your Standard Operating Procedures manual establishes the minimum and corporate standards for customer experience. Underscore that if they can find authentic ways to exceed those expectations, the benefit to everyone involved will be huge.

Team members must be trained, encouraged, and rewarded for building their own relationships, in their own ways, using their own personalities and connections with certain customers. People don't want to do business with businesses; they want to do business with people. If you are looking for one place to start formalizing your positive feedback system, training is a great place to start.

Manufacture Repeat Business

Coffee shops figured this out a long time ago: loyalty can be made tangible. Loyalty cards, where you get a tenth cup of coffee for free after 9 visits, have been a staple on the coffee scene for over a decade. Their popularity is fading now, but that is because in many cases they are not implemented properly. Loyalty cards are still effective. Starbucks is still using them to enormous benefit to their business.

Create incentives for customers to come back. Combining your data collection program with a loyalty program (and they *should* be connected), gives you opportunities to create special events like anniversary sales for loyal or A-list customers. When you harvest information like birthdays, you can invite customers back for special deals on their birthday. Not every business can do this for every customer, but most businesses can do it for their A-lists: write a handwritten note, or even pick up the phone.

This is a natural extension of the contact harvesting and loyalty program tactics.

A client of mine who owns a shoe store trains her sales staff to hand out a business card with their name on it at the end of each successful transaction, and walk the customer to the sales counter where they ask the customer if they are on the store's mailing list. In a carefully scripted message the employee economically spells out the advantages of belonging to their loyalty program. If the customer agrees to provide contact information, the sales associate records the information and promises to stay in touch. Of course the customer has heard a line like that a hundred times before. So imagine their surprise when two weeks later the phone rings and it is the sales associate calling to check on how the shoes are working out, and if there are any concerns the customer has!

Flash Point

In the whole area of harvesting contact information, whether for a loyalty program or for other communication purposes, be aware of the privacy laws in your jurisdiction. The laws around the acceptable collection and appropriate storage and use of information like email addresses and birthdays are increasingly protective of the consumer - as they should be. However, consumers can still give their willing consent to provide any of this information when the correct disclosures are made. Customer contact information is valuable enough that making sure you have dotted your i's and crossed your t's in understanding and abiding by the rules, is worth it.

♫

Provide A Great Experience

Not just great *products*, not even great service. A great *experience*. Examine every aspect of how your customers experience your business, and try to find a way to make it fun, different, low-stress, and remarkable. Remember the customer experience cycle:

you want to feed that positive feedback loop from the moment a potential customer first hears about you.

Examine everything, from the way you answer the phone, to the layout of your store, to the way customers pay and leave.

Everything should reinforce your brand, and give your customers something positive to talk about. You can try all the other customer relationship-building tactics, but if the actual time doing business with you does not create an incentive to come back, it's all just window dressing.

Customer experience is to business what *musicianship* is to music: the whole point. Customer experience is what every other part of this book ultimately seeks to feed. Done right, remarkable customer experiences ultimately feed everything else. Just another feedback loop!

♫

Journal Intermission

- Think about every major step on the customer experience cycle: awareness; deciding you have a solution to their problem; concluding a sale; follow-through. Come up with one new way to do something remarkable at each of the four stages, that all connect. Perhaps it has something to do with the name of your business, or the nature of your services or products. Be creative. How will the way you follow through after a sale connect with the way they first heard about you? How can you make both moments more memorable?

- Write a list of 10 things your customers would find valuable based on their interest in your products or services. Use the story of the toy store I shared earlier as an example of this.

♫♫♫

Scene 2: Life After The Sale: Follow-up

Performance Notes
*Two things reveal the true heart of a business:
how they treat their customers after the cash register rings,
and how they deal with mistakes and crises.*

Band Camp Performance:

The one-night-stand mentality that loses interest when the cash register rings; mistaking the value of a commodity for the value of a relationship.

Great Performance:

Making customers feel absolutely confident that they matter as much after the cash register rings, as they did before.

♫

If there is one true magical force in customer retention it is follow-through. Yet if there is one area in the marketing of a small business that is as neglected as it is powerful, it is also follow-through. You would think it is a state secret! We touched on follow-through earlier, but it is so important I want to dedicate a whole scene to it here.

How often have you called a business with the intention of purchasing a product or service, only to wait 3 days for a return phone call? Or wait 9 days for an email? If the business wanted to broadcast the message that they were too busy to do business, message received.

The heart of a Great Performance by a small business is customer retention. The heart of customer retention is follow-up and follow-through. To create that Great Performance in follow-through and retention you need a few key elements in place.

As you learned earlier, we have to manage our relationships with our customers in the cycle I call the *customer experience spiral*. We divide the customer experience into four phases: awareness, confirming you can solve their problem, purchase, and follow-through. There is a lot more to it than that (read the work of John Jantsch or Steve Yastrow if you really want to master the art of this area of marketing), but that is enough foundation to build on.

What separates Great Performances from Band Camp performances is which part of the cycle you focus on.

Businesses in Band Camp throw all of their resources at the beginning of the cycle: promoting, advertising, enticing, promising, persuading, seducing. They might then take things one step further and insist on this thing called customer service during the actual purchase, as the cash register is ringing. But then things quickly fall apart. Band Camp businesses have no staying power, and no mature sense of commitment to sustaining the quality of customer experience through the whole customer experience spiral.

For a truly Great Performance of the standing-ovation and roses-flying-through-the-air kind, you have to manage *every part* of that experience equally well. When you want to focus on where you can make the biggest difference and where your competitors consistently stumble on, it is in *post-purchase follow-through*.

When businesses focus only on the work of getting a sale, it is hard not to see it as anything other than getting the money and running.

No number of *U Matter to Us* posters stuck around the building can dispel the sense that the only time I truly matter is before I fork over my money. The moment I have, it's like the light goes off! It feels like someone saying, "That was good for me, was that good for you?" As they are already half way out the door. Wow. That's sincere.

A business can say *it cares* all it wants, but unless its actions *after* the sale match its rhetoric, those are just empty words - and customers pick up that message quickly.

Doing The Band Camp Spiral

Once customers pick up that signal they are just a commodity themselves, as they did in the Band Camp case study about Campbell's Pharmacy, the spiral now turns the wrong way.

The Band Camp negative customer experience spiral goes like this:

- You lure me with promises and raise my expectations,
- You fail to deliver on those expectations and I have a poor experience,
- You can't woo me back on your original promise or my experience of your business, so you woo me back with discounts and specials,
- The discounts and promotions erode your profit margin, making it even harder for you to deliver a great customer experience.
- You discount further to bring me back...

We can all see where this goes. The moment you trade customer experience for discounts, you have just stepped into the very scary world of the BBSs: Big Box Stores, or the Big Bad Stores, whatever your sense of them is. When you discount to make up for poor customer experience by going to more discounts, you move into their sandbox.

If all you have to offer is a discount to keep your customers out of the BBS's, you better have very deep pockets and enormous purchasing power because they can outspend you and outlast you.

♫

Turning It Around

It's not hard to see that focusing on shaping a great customer experience and building a positive customer experience cycle is far preferable to going head-to-head with Wal-Mart on pricing. So how do you go about creating a Great Performance based on remarkable follow-up and follow-through?

Curtains Up!

If your customers aren't thrilled with their experience of your actual products or services, then the rest of the cycle is academic. Your customers came to you in the first place because they had a need or a problem they believed you could solve. *It is all about them.* So set reasonable expectations during the promotional phase of the cycle, then blow them out of the water when it comes time to deliver. After that, it's paint-by-numbers: get in touch and stay in touch.

A Rich CRM Database

The more you know about your customers the better you can take care of them. That doesn't just mean information you collect at the cash register. Anything and everything you can do to know your customers' desires, concerns, habits, and networks will enable you to build a relationship on something more than a name and a postal or zip code.

This is where encouraging employees to go out of their way to connect with customers, to form unique relationships within the larger framework of the relationship with the business, can be a powerful tool. It is tough to manage 1000 relationships well, but it gets easier when that task is divided up between 10 employees, each responsible for their own list of customers.

The more your customers feel like you really understand them, the deeper the connection.

Social Media

Yep. I bet you were wondering when we would get here. Well, now's the time. In the world of business the social networks like Facebook, Twitter, or LinkedIn can play three possible roles:

1. **Influence-building.** Social media is playing an increasingly important role for independent professionals, solo-preneurs, and consultants looking to build a career that involves business-to-business (B2B) services, public speaking, or building a client base. Speaker's Bureaus may still ask if you have published a book, as they have for decades, but increasingly they are also asking for the number of Facebook Fans your professional page has. One of the ways I decide whether you can solve my problem (phase 2 of the customer-experience cycle) is by finding out if you are an expert in your field. When I Google you and find you have a blog on the subject I am looking for help in, or a strong LinkedIn presence, or a resource-rich and active Facebook Page, my confidence in your ability will go up.

   Speaking of an active Facebook Page, that is another area of influence. It is not just about expertise, it is also about *what others say* about you. As humans we are naturally more comfortable when we can take cues from those around us (a principle in psychology and sociology called *social proof*). We believe a restaurant might be good because other humans are already packed in there and having a good time. Social media can exert the same kind of social influence. It is one thing for us to speak well of our products and services, but when our network on Facebook, Twitter, LinkedIn, Google Local or other platforms is freely and publicly saying good things about us, that is a very powerful form of influence.

2. **Lead generation.** Social networks can help get the word out directly to potential customers. In particular social media

can play an important role in amplifying traditional word-of-mouth (WOM) marketing. Where one friend used to be able to tell one other friend about your services, now they can tell thousands. You can use social media to market and promote your business directly, as long as it is done appropriately. How that works is the subject of another book, but suffice it to say that if you get it right, social media can be a powerful lead generation tool.

3. **Customer retention.** This is something social networks are brilliant at. One of the biggest challenges in larger organizations today is to maintain that common touch so necessary for maintaining great customer relationships. How do you exercise the common touch when you have thousands or tens-of-thousands of customers? One powerful tool in helping get this job done is social media. A business's reach and ability to monitor and connect with the broad base of its customers is greater now than at any other time in history. In a phrase, social media can be a powerful tool in the development of your follow-through with customers.

♬

Social platforms let you stay in touch in a way impossible to imagine a decade ago. Further, you can weave your business into the fabric of your customers' lives to insert front-of-mind and high-conversion incentives exactly where they will get noticed.

Social channels also give you an unprecedented ability to monitor your brand and the desires, obsessions, and stresses of your customers (which you can use in turn to enrich your CRM database). As a business owner it is important to understand sales and marketing concepts like qualifying, conversion, and closing. Social media can be very effective tools with the first two.

Qualifying is the process of ensuring the marketing resources you are investing in are with someone who is likely to purchase.

An *unqualified* consumer is one who is neither motivated to buy in general or who is not attracted to your offer particularly.

Conversion is the process of getting a customer to act in some desired way: picking up the phone, downloading some software, subscribing to a newsletter, or making a purchase.

Closing happens when the wallet comes out, or the contract is signed. Social media do not usually have a direct role to play in this.

Because social networks are filled with people who know each other (or at least know *of* each other) to one degree or another, there is a greater potential for generating positive word of mouth.

You can build social proof faster amongst people of like mind. This is central to the concept of *brand communities:* the idea that there are groups of people who love BMWs or Jeeps or California wines or certain brands of athletic wear, and those people see themselves as having something in common with others loyal to that brand.

These are people who are happy to share positively about the product or service, and even become what are called brand evangelists. It is not hard to see how a Facebook page dedicated to a popular brand (like Starbucks, Coca Cola, or Victoria's Secret) could be used to market directly to highly qualified consumers. Prior to social media, there was no other way to keep such large communities of fans so close at hand and so engaged in generating positive influence on the market.

Performance Note
*Email newsletters have a better ROI
than any of the social networks.*

Electronic Newsletters

Another powerful tool that allows you to easily communicate

with your customers is the electronic newsletter. Using your CRM database to create a mailing list, you can send out weekly or monthly newsletters.

Newsletters are not, strictly speaking, social media because they are not interactive, yet this is also the thing that gives them their unique power. Any social media site is largely passive: it sits and waits for you to go to it before it can work its magic. A newsletter is active in that, with permission, you can send it directly to a person's inbox at a time of your choosing.

Many novices to the world of Web-based or social marketing are surprised and disappointed to learn that even a good email newsletter campaign may only have an open rate of 20% (the percentage of people who open the email instead of sending it directly to the trash). However, when compared to other conversion rates, this is spectacular. For example the click-through rate on banner advertisements that you see near the top of many websites, is less than 2%.

If you go out of your way to discover what truly interests your customers, and provide content that addresses this, as well as providing *subscriber-only* incentives and special offers, newsletters are a great way of staying in touch with your customers after the sale.

A Schedule And A Budget

Without a schedule or a budget, you don't have a plan, you have an idea. Good follow-up requires a modest budget, and a generous allocation of time. The more detail (about your customers) you want to leverage, the more time-consuming the system. Tailored communications, anything personalized or handwritten, telephone calls, etc., all take time. Social media take time. Someone has to be allocated the time, and the budget has to be there to pay them.

Of particular importance is a clear follow-through and retention schedule. Everything from personal contacts with Triple-A-List customers to generalized newsletter blasts should be scheduled into the life of your organization.

As with so many other areas of business, structure and consistency matter in creating a great performance in customer follow-through.

Incentives

Being a return customer should come with privileges. We all want to be recognized and valued. Great bartenders understand this when they ask you, "Will it be your usual, Sheila?" Coffee shops understand this with their free coffee with every 10th cup cards. Rewarding a loyal customer not only gives them a reason for coming back, it makes them feel good about coming back.

Journal Intermission

- Write down 3 small things you could do in your place of business or in your day-to-day interactions with your customers to make their experience of that moment more memorable.

- Take some time to search for and look through the websites, Facebook Pages, Twitter feeds, etc., of businesses who do the same thing you do (AKA 'the competition'). Write down a list of things you think you could borrow or steal to make your own social presence more interesting or valuable to your customers.

- Based on what you know about your business and your customers, do you think social media would be most effective in the area of building influence, generating leads, or sustaining relationships? What is one platform (Twitter, Facebook, etc.) you could use and one thing you could do on that platform to improve your effectiveness in the area you have identified?

♫♫♫

SCENE 3: The Performers And The Audience

Band Camp Performance:

Assuming everyone knows what matters; all talk and no walk when it comes to putting people first.

Great Performances:

Sharing the goals and objectives with your team, and letting them figure out how to use their strengths to work out the details.

♫

Performance Note

"Everyone has an invisible sign hanging from their neck saying, 'Make me feel important.' Never forget this message when working with people."
Mary Kay Ash

It's Personal

In the Great Performance of your business, your people are the actors, the musicians, the dancers who are the stars. No one in an orchestra or a ballet company is called a resource. They are the performers.

As I stayed largely clear of advertising and promotion in the first two scenes of this book, I will stay away from *human resources* in the next few scenes. It is true that people in a business are a resource. They are one of the 3 (and only 3) resources that a business has: time, people, and money. But that is language we want to be careful with. People are so much more than just a passive resource like time and money. They don't just sit there and wait for you to use them as you would the other two resources.

The people in your business: your partners, employees, staff, team—whatever language you use—are resources, but they are also so much more than that. They are the only truly magical ingredient in your business. The people on your team can bring passion, energy, commitment, vision, endurance, leadership, initiative, intuition, selflessness, and so much more into the picture. Neither time nor money can make that claim.

So these scenes are not about human resources. They are about the powerful magic of people.

♫

You Say People Matter. Can You Prove It?

People are at the heart of everything we do in business. While customers are the must-have to create a viable business, a great team is the must-have to create a Great Performance in a business! You wouldn't know that to watch a lot of businesses.

How do I know when something is a *real* priority in a business? I check schedules and budgets. What I see are time and money for marketing, for new stuff, for all kinds of things, but almost nothing *for people* beyond the basic cost of labour.

I have watched as businesses bought new equipment, started new marketing campaigns, moved into new markets, and planned new directions, all before identifying who is going to manage, run, or lead the new reality. The message these businesses are sending out is that the business or the idea or the equipment is what matters, and the people to run them are an afterthought.

"But wait!" you say, "Doesn't it say in Gerber's *The E-Myth* people don't matter if you have great systems? Can't a monkey run something if the system is designed well enough?" First of all that is not what The E-Myth says. When you read this seminal book (and anyone starting a small business should), you will see that Michael Gerber does indeed value the contributions of people. Gerber does overstate the systems side of the equation. In the running narrative about a pie-maker in the book, there is the strong message that with good enough manuals you don't need great *bakers*. I think that is simply not true.

Performance Note
A business without great performers
is just an address with a heating bill.

Thinking that great systems render great performers superfluous is true only for a limited number of positions in a limited number of businesses, for example low-level employees of businesses for whom competing on price is a primary strategy. It works for entry-level floor positions in big-box stores, or food assembly workers in fast-food outlets. But no manual ever written will turn an 18-year-old burger flipper into a line-cook in a Michelin 3-Star restaurant.

That is not to say systems are not important; in fact, one of the things that makes a restaurant a 3-Star contender is an absolutely rigorous adherence to systems. In a truly great restaurant, meals must be great every time in exactly the same way, at exactly the same cost. Those systems and operating procedures are there to *support* great talent, not make it unnecessary.

People have to come first. You can build the shiniest new store on the planet, but if you don't have the people there to make it everything it could be, it's just a street address with a heating bill.

♫

Building a Team for Great Performances

There are hundreds of things a business needs to do right in building the team it needs for a Great Performance. This is not a human resources manual; this is a handbook of a few key approaches that in my experience are the difference between a Great Performance and getting booed off the stage. Here we go.

A Team Is An Investment, Not An Expense

When doing the cost-benefit calculations to build their teams, too many business owners ask themselves only one question: "How much is this gonna cost me?"

That approach to team building is pure Band Camp and pretty much guarantees your profitability will never be what it should, you will never escape the stresses and limitations of personally being on the tools every day, and your business will never return the blood, sweat, tears, time, and money you put into it. You won't make Broadway because your band will never leave the garage.

What is missing in this cost-fixated thinking is the strategic dimension: developing a team to improve the performance of your business, not just continue the status quo. Adding the right team-member should do one or all of three things: increase revenues, increase profitability, or create strategic possibilities.

Hiring can increase profit? How does that work? There are many ways, and I will give you one by way of another mini Band-Camp performance story:

> Susie is an amazing sales person. She is a virtuoso. She is dedicated, experienced, and an amazing performer. Every hour she is in the presence of customers, doing what she does best, she generates thousands of dollars in revenue.

How does her boss handle Susie? Does he go out of his way to build a structure around her to let her perform without distractions? Does he maximize her talents and her time in front of customers? Nope. He structures things so that Susie spends 40% to 60% of her time doing paperwork and tending to operational minutiae.

In the performing arts world, this would be the equivalent of an orchestra taking their First Violinist, and having her spend most of her time filling out grant applications.

In short, to save $15 per hour on a support person, the employer is prepared to walk away from thousands of dollars each day by hobbling his star performer.

Pretty bad right? It gets worse. Sometimes Susie owns the business. Too often Suzie is not an employee, she is you.

I worked with one business owner whose unique skills as an artist were required to complete a product that generated $1,000 in revenues per day. Because of a bad experience with a bookkeeper, she spent every Monday doing her own books. She spent a full day doing what a competent bookkeeper could have accomplished in an hour or two—and for a lot less than $1,000! Needless to say, when this business owner became a client and I became aware of the situation, that insanity quickly came to an end.

You know the saying you have to spend money to make money? While not universally true, it is an important concept. Building a team by weaving in the right people is exactly that: a growth strategy. Spending the right money on the right people will make you more money.

We'll explore this in greater depth next in Scenes 4 and 5.

Play Your Positions

Designing A Strengths-Alignment Strategy

This is a concept that is fundamental to the worlds of sports and the performing arts, but barely acknowledged in most businesses: everyone on a team performs their best when they are playing their position. In the theatre you don't see many comic stars playing serious tragic roles. In sports you don't see keepers playing midfield, or quarterbacks doing much tackling.

Yet in business I see that all the time. It is understandable at the beginning a business and its team have to be many things to many people (or to many tasks). The more quickly we can move away from that Band-Camp practice, the more quickly we will be playing in the Great-Performance leagues.

As quickly as your cash flow allows, strip nonessential roles and responsibilities from every member of your team and assign it to someone who can do it better, faster, or cheaper.

We call this a strengths-alignment strategy because it is the job of every great manager to do one thing before all else: align the strengths and talents of team members with the vision and the needs of the organization. You must develop a strategy to ensure the people in your business are doing what they do best. Every degree you are off that path, you are wasting resources and losing momentum in your quest for the Great Performance.

Great people in the right positions will keep your business aimed squarely at achieving that Great Performance of your dreams.

♫

Journal Intermission

- Look over your budget or financial statements. Do you spend any money on training or anything else to develop your team beyond the basic costs of labour (wages, benefits, etc.)? If not, what commitment can you make to spend something on building your team?

- Look over your schedule. Do you spend regular time on training or any form of team development? If not what is one step you can take to make a regular commitment to this area?

♫♫♫

SCENE 4: Always Be Recruiting

Band Camp Performance:

Scrambling to hire people every time someone leaves your team; treating employees purely as cost centers.

Great Performance:

Broadcasting the message, "We are open for talent" 24 hours a day, 365 days a year; acting on the understanding that great employees will always return more than you invest in them.

♫

Performance Note

If you start your recruiting process when you need someone, you have left it too long.

When is the best time to be recruiting? Not when you need someone!

Far too often I have watched as employers sail merrily along on the belief that no one ever quits, or gets sick, or moves to a new community. Then, when one of those *totally unforeseeable* things happens, they fire up the recruitment engines in a panic. Out go the newspaper ads, in come the candidates. No time for fussy stuff like reference checks. No time to ask why when every other person in their trade is currently working, the candidate happens to be footloose and fancy free.

And we're stunned when they don't work out!

If you start your recruiting process when you need someone, you have left it too long. Even when you are not *hiring* you should be *recruiting*. What's the difference? Hiring is the one-time bringing someone on board and offering them a job. Recruiting is the ongoing process of letting the world know you are open for talent, and holding regular interviews to find that talent, *even if you don't currently have an opening.*

A Brief Lesson In Probability

Why? It's a classic probability problem: if you take two *unrelated* probabilities, you *multiply* them together to get the probability of them *both* happening.

> **Example:** I have a 10% chance of finding money in my pocket and I have a 10% chance of finding a parking spot where I need one. This means I have a 1% chance of finding money in my pocket *and* finding a parking spot (.1 x .1 = .01)

How does that work when you look at recruiting?

For starters, the probability of you needing talent at a certain time, and the probability of a person with the right talents to fill the position, are unrelated. Great talent doesn't time her appearance with your needs. Just because you are looking for someone doesn't mean all across the city just the right people are quitting their jobs to come and apply for yours!

It really works like this: if great talent is available 10% of the time, and you are looking for talent 10% of the time, *the possibility of both happening at the same time is 1% of the time.* That's just not good enough when your Great Performance is dependent on the strengths alignment strategy. Here is how to do it right.

Performance Note

If I can't find it on your schedule and as a line item in your budget, it doesn't exist. It is a wish, not a plan.

Get The Word Out

Get the word out on the street through your current employees and your customers: if you have what it takes, our business wants to talk to you. Have your management team make it a priority.

Create Casting Calls, Not Job Descriptions

Forget "Help Wanted". You want "Looking for Crazy Talent" or "If you are an amazing [fill in the skill here], we want you!" on your website, on Craigslist, periodically on your social media channels. If you are creating a Great Performance, you are looking for talent, not help.

This is as much of a marketing exercise as anything you do to sell your products and services. Have fun with this, switch it up, and for goodness sake stay away from anything that looks like a Human Resources specialist has written it (even if one did)!

Employers are always looking for the best they can get, but few are prepared to put the best they can do into that search. Remember the old GIGO adage: garbage in, garbage out. If you want remarkable employees write a remarkable job ad!

Set Aside Time Each Month For Interviews

I've said it before and I'll repeat myself later just so we're clear: *if I can't find it on your schedule and as a line item in your budget, it doesn't exist.* If you are going to take building a great team seriously, and you understand that always recruiting is a key part of that, then carve out a chunk of precious time and money for it.

Interview In Teams

Have at least one team member with you when you interview. Have someone there to kick you under the table if you are heading into hot water asking stupid questions (and yes, there are such things) like, "So you're married, I'm assuming you're not planning on getting pregnant in the next 10 years?" Also, one person needs to be interviewing and another observing and recording. Few people have the skill to run the interview, take notes, and really observe the candidate all at the same time.

Think Like A Casting Agent

Good casting agents not only have an eye for great talent, they also know they are only as valuable as their contact lists. For really key positions, directors and casting agents don't rely on cattle calls (general auditions) but have a living list of great talent to call when the opportunity presents itself. Set up a filing cabinet drawer or a computer folder with all the promising resumes you have received.

This part is important because that filing cabinet drawer (or secure computer directory) is the nerve center of all your hard recruiting work. This is the place you turn to when that key employee just up and leaves you. This is your trove of power tools you can call up when business gets too big to handle. It's like that chocolate bar in your desk: it's just good to know it's there; and when you need it, it's awesome!

A Star Is Born

When superstar talent walks through your door, hire them. Even if you don't need them. We have already explained why in the explanation of probabilities above: it is improbable a superstar will walk through your door when it is a good time to hire them. They will walk through your door when there are a dozen reasons why right now *is not* a good time. That's just the odds.

Performance Note
The definition of a superstar:
a person you can't afford not to hire.

The most common objections are "We can't afford them" and "I don't have a position for them."The response to both objections is simple: true talent always returns more value to the organization than you invest in it. If you bring them in and they don't either earn you money or save you money in excess of what you are paying them, they are not a superstar.

The definition of real superstar talent is: *a candidate you can't afford not to hire.* Here is another reason to hire them: if you don't, your competition will. If they are a real superstar, that's going to hurt. The Jimi Hendrixs or Meryl Streeps of the world can be a part of your project, or you can let them walk out of the door to be a part of someone else's. Your call.

♫

Journal Intermission

- If you are an employer, review the positions on your staff. Write down a list of positions. After each one, write down what would happen to your business if the employee currently holding that position left tomorrow.

- Pick one of the key positions and write the most attractive, compelling, and fun job ad you can for that position. As with any form of marketing, what the customer (in this case a potential employee) wants matters more than what you want. Consider compelling benefits like money, time, a social life, responsibility, opportunity, career path, security, and so on. Write it as if you were trying to attract a 19-year old. Write it as if you were trying to attract a retiree. Write it as if you were trying to attract the next Bill Gates or Steve Jobs.

♫♫♫

SCENE 5: The Power Of Positive Feedback

Performance Note
"Feedback is the breakfast of champions."
Ken Blanchard

Band Camp Performance:

Assuming everyone knows what matters; using fear, intimidation, and micromanagement to get results. Being a boss instead of a leader.

Great Performance:

Sharing the goals and objectives with your team, and letting them figure out how to use their strengths to work out the details. Providing positive feedback at each instance of individual performance that moves the business forward.

♫

Speaking of superstars, let's start with the most important one: you. Your best offense in the battle to thrive in tough times is to be a superstar yourself. Be the superstar manager your staff and customers need you to be.

Management is a craft and a skill, and there are Band Camp managers and Great Performance managers. Being a superstar manager in a small business is all about one simple thing: *positive feedback*. If you don't have a systematic, consistent positive feedback program, I guarantee two things: your employees don't know enough about what you really want, and sub-par performance and staff turnover is going to keep you in Band Camp.

While few business owners think of it this way, positive feedback is the only way of *guaranteeing* your employees know where you are taking the business and what they can best do to help get you there."Wait," you're probably thinking, "all I have to do to achieve a Great Performance in my business is pat people on the back, and give them a bonus once a year? That's a lot of horse shit, and I'm going to skip this section and get to the chapters about selling more stuff!"

Let's start by erasing one thing from your mind right now: positive feedback is not about backslaps and telling everyone they did a "great job" in a sloppy indiscriminate smear of feel-good.

No. Great positive feedback is a rigorous system that is as precise and as effective (and as challenging to use correctly) as a high-tech medical instrument. The operative word to help you understand the focus here is *system*. This is something you design carefully and execute religiously. The reason this system is called positive feedback is not because it makes people feel good (although done right, it sure does that), it is because you are providing *feedback* on effective performance to get more of the same performance. That is the heart of positive feedback. People get hung up on the word positive and stop listening. They never get to the feedback part, and don't understand the origin of the phrase. Allow me some technical background here.

Positively Technical

Let's start with a revelation: from an experiential perspective positive feedback is not always positive!

Have you ever been at a concert where a squealing sound starts coming from the speakers in the hall, which quickly becomes an unbearably loud howl? That's positive feedback. Bank or stock runs where more and more people take their money out of a bank or stock faster and faster? That's positive feedback too. Positive feedback occurs when one part of a system amplifies or causes to repeat another part of that system, which in turn amplifies the first part again. In the case of the howling speakers at the concert, the amplifiers in the sound system take the signal from the microphone, make it louder, the mic picks it up again and feeds it back to the amplifiers, which again make it louder. This goes round and round until, in a few seconds, you have the squeal of feedback.

Experts also refer to this process as self-reinforcing feedback, which is a more accurate description and gets away from that word positive people get hung up on. We'll stick with *positive feedback* though, because it is so widely understood in team development circles.

We Want More Of The Good Stuff

So how does understanding this get us closer to a Great Performance? The answers is positive feedback systems give us more of what we want. In designing a business for a Great Performance, we want to:

* Find a way to highlight desired behaviors;
* Amplify them;
* And have them happen over and over again in an ever-increasing, self-reinforcing way, just like the sound in the conference hall, only without the squeal.

♫

You Go First

The first part to get this system right isn't your employees' job, it's yours.

Performance Note

"When you take a pitch and line it somewhere, it's like you've thought of something and put it there with beautiful clarity."

Reggie Jackson

Clarify Objectives

Your first job is to clarify your objectives—and then clarify them again. Your employees can't tune their performance or focus their resources if they don't know exactly where you want to go. Be sure you are absolutely clear yourself, then communicate your vision and objectives to the rest of your team.

Repeat yourself as often as you have to, and constantly check for understanding. If you don't do this part right, everything afterwards collapses into the mushy pile of feel-good manure most people think about when they hear the phrase "positive feedback." If you can't communicate to each employee exactly where you are going, and what *their* role is in getting you there, true positive feedback becomes impossible. The initial signal is missing. There is nothing to amplify.

Connect The Wires

After you have communicated the objectives, make it clear to each employee exactly how the skills and attitudes you hired them for mesh with those objectives. Remind employees that you hired them because you saw a unique combination of abilities, attitudes, and behaviours (you did, right?) that were a potential asset for the business.

Be explicit when you connect their skills to what's needed. Here's what you say: *"This is where I see the organization going. These are the unique strengths you have. This is how I want you to apply those skills."*

Now The Magic Happens

When you "catch" a team member contributing their strengths to the overall performance in the way you suggested, amplify the signal. This is where you get to be positive. You say something like, "That was fantastic. That was exactly what we talked about, and I would love to see more of that."

Performance Note
Positive feedback is not praise.
It is amplifying the value of someone making the right choice.

Here are some further guidelines about how amplifying the signal works.

Be Precise But Be Generous

For goodness sake, don't wait for fireworks, or Christmas, or signs from the stars before you recognize an employee for good performance as you have defined it.

We have defined the goal as an *employee using their strengths to achieve the objectives of the business.* You are using feedback to confirm for the employee they are headed in the right direction, to encourage and nurture more of that behaviour.

The first time you "catch" an employee doing it right, comment positively. And the second time. And a third time. If you haven't provided positive feedback to every employee in the course of the week, either you aren't doing this right, or they are not doing their job right. Either way, you have to address it.

Be Systematic

In life, *anything worth doing is worth doing right,* the saying goes.

In business, anything worth doing is worth planning, tracking, evaluating, and writing down!

Document conversations about objectives and about desired behaviours and performance.

Use checklists to track your own performance in providing positive feedback. As a goal, you could check in with each employee at least once a day and look for opportunities to provide positive feedback. How would you track your own performance in this?

Put It In Writing

Document both the goals of the organization and the process you use for connecting and rewarding desired performances. This document will become a valuable part of the management guidelines for your Standard Operating Procedures (more about that to come).

Use The Network Effect

In sociology, the network effect (or *bandwagon effect*) is a description of how the more people do something, the more it is of interest to others. This is social positive feedback. For example, the more people are jammed into a restaurant, the more we want to be in there. The more that people use a certain piece of software (email or a social network), the more the rest of us feel pressure to jump on the bandwagon or we risk feeling like we are missing out. This effect is part of a functioning positive feedback system.

On a healthy team, the more members watch you reward certain kinds of behaviour, the more the rest buy in. We've all seen it: when a leader is overheard making a positive comment about how they appreciate that someone is always on time, most of us feel compelled to work harder to be on time ourselves!

Designed appropriately, your feedback results in positive returns for the organization and the team, and even more people see the value and want to get on board. It is human instinct to want to be a part of something that is clearly positive and feeds our own prospects at the same time.

Performance Note
Celebrate publicly, criticize privately.

Use perks. Positive feedback for desirable behaviour is, and should be, verbal and informal. You are letting the employee know they are on the right track, and broadcasting to those around them to leverage the network effect.

Don't shy away from material perks for remarkable performance. If someone's efforts have added value to the organization, share some of that benefit with them.

♬

Journal Intermission

- Write down the top 3 objectives for your business this quarter.

- Think of your key employees. Write down their names, and beside each one write down a few of their biggest strengths, and how each strength could contribute to one or more of your 3 objectives.

- For each employee on your list also note what an above-and-beyond performance would look like. You have a much better chance of seeing it if you know what it is you are looking for.

♫♫♫

Scene 6: Employees Care for Customers

"The very underpinning of Madison Avenue is based on the notion that you are really two people: The person you are, and the person you want to be. The dreams and fantasies that luxury marketing weaves only want to talk to person number two."

The Age of Persuasion (CBC) Terry O'Reilly

Band Camp Performance:

Thinking you, as the owner, are the only one who can really talk to your customers; thinking you can have one set of values for your customers and another for your employees.

Great Performance:

Acting on the understanding your employees are the most important part of your business.

♫

Which matter more, your employees or your customers?

The truth is it's a chicken and egg question. Without any customers you wouldn't have a business; without *happy* customers, you won't have a business for long. Your employees are key to ensuring you have happy customers. They make it possible for you to keep your customers happy. Conversely, poor employee behaviour is by far the single biggest reason customers don't return to a business.

Companies like Southwest Airlines and Westjet figured out

this connection a long time ago. Southwest famously turned the business world on its head in the 1970s when it declared it would rank employees ahead of customers and shareholders in order of priority to the company.

You need happy customers to keep the doors open, and you need great employees to keep your customers happy.

Understanding this sequence is very important. A business owner's focus must be on employees before customers because that is the long and sustainable view to take in growing a business. Advertising may get you customers, but only your employees can help you keep them. It goes deeper: in creating a Great Performance, it is critical you remove yourself from being the *first and only* point of contact for your customers. Success in business is staggeringly difficult if you try to do everything yourself, and as you grow you simply won't be able to.

Performance Note

If you are the only person who knows everything and does everything in your business, then you are more self-employed than business owner. What if you get hit by a bus?

When business owners hear the phrase "work on the business rather than in the business" most think working on the business means excluding things like operations (baking, painting, wrenching, driving) or finances (bookkeeping). When it comes to caring for customers they still see themselves as the first and only point of contact. They are prepared to let go of a lot, but not that.

While it is true managing the overall quality of customer experience is a critically important job for a business owner, that does not mean you need to be behind the counter. As long as you see yourself as the only one who gets it enough to interact with customers, especially the "important" ones, you are creating a serious restriction on your business's ability to grow.

You can only see so many customers in a day; every hour you spend with customers is one hour you are not spending on the health and well-being of your business as a whole.

Furthermore, as you will learn in the last section of this book, if a potential buyer or investor in your business learns you are the only one whom customers turn to for key sales or problem solving, that will become a stroke against you. Who wants to invest in a business where the most critical aspects of the customer experience rely on the health and presence of one person? What if you get hit by a bus?

Customer sales and service are often the last and most difficult things for me to get business owners to let go of. I have to pry their fingers off those controls one finger at a time. Caring for your business is your responsibility. Caring for your customers is your team's responsibility.

That said, there are some critically important components you must design to achieve that Great Performance in customer experiences. The most important of all is retention. I see businesses make this mistake more consistently than any other in the area of marketing, it is focusing attention and resources on acquiring new customers at the expense of retaining their existing ones.

Performance Note
Be a keeper not a getter.

The value of retention applies as much to your team members as to your customers. Employee turnover is as costly as customers who only come in once.

To drive home the point in another way, look at the models we have in music, dance, and theatre. Can you imagine expecting a superior performance from a band, orchestra, dance company, or theatre where the artists are constantly leaving and being replaced? Or where there is no focus on developing a fan base?

Where each performance is marketed from scratch, aiming to put a totally new audience in the seats each time? Insane, right? Retain your great performers, and build your fan base. These are non-negotiable and separate Band Camp performances from truly Great Performances.

♫

Journal Intermission

- Write down the top 3 things that define great customer service for your business.

- How would you communicate and train an employee in providing those 3 things? What would you say to the employee?

Act I Summary

People are the core of your business. Yes, you need great systems to support your customers and your employees, but that is what those systems are: supporting roles.

For truly Great Performances you need a great script, but without the actors, the script lies center stage, in a pool of light, not doing a damn thing. You need actors and a support team, and you need an audience that has come to expect nothing but the best from you. In return for fulfilling those expectations, they return every evening and fill the house.

The two groups we focus on in retention—employees and customers—are intimately woven together. You cannot build a great customer retention program without a great employee retention program. Only engaged, loyal employees cooperatively generating a vibrant organizational culture, can create the kind of customer experience that keeps people coming back.

Finding good people for your team, and finding great customers who truly click with what you have to offer, is important. Keeping them matters even more. Be a keeper, not just a getter. A Great Performance by your business is not possible if your staff turnover is too high, or if you are spending most of your budget on acquiring new customers and almost nothing to keep them. Review where you are putting your time and your money. More than what you say, where you spend these resources reveals where your real priorities are.

Spend your time and money developing a culture that values initiative, risk-taking, and relationships. Always be recruiting for that next great superstar; when you have them, show them where you want the organization to go, and ask them how they can use their talents to get you there—then get out of the way.

Spend more time and money on building relationships with the customers you have than acquiring new ones. If you do it right your fans will become brand evangelists and do your promoting for you. Great performances require that everyone know their part. That kind of mastery is possible only if everyone sticks around.

♫♫♫

Master Class: Designing A Truly People-First Business

Performance Note

"To put your son in a position to care about winning and not to prepare him is wrong!"
Bruce Pandolfini (Ben Kingsley)
in *Searching for Bobby Fischer*

Check the boxes as you go through this. These points are not optional. There is no Great Performance until you have checked off 100% of the boxes!

The ***Do This Now*** items are marked to indicate if you do not have these in place in your business, forget the list, and do these first!

The day-to-day execution of these items would take another book to describe. That might be coming. In the meantime, hire a good business coach to guide you through these steps.

☐

1. Write and review your mission statement. *Do This Now*

_____

_____

_____

☐

2. Declare your business objectives for this year. *Do This Now*

_____

_____

_____

☐

3. Meet with your team and/or your coach to create a customer experience vision and charter. *Do This Now*

_____

_____

_____

☐

4. Set out the non-negotiables as written standards, especially how mistakes and complaints are dealt with.

_____

_____

_____

☐

5. Build the culture:

a. Work with your team to write the delivery model to make the Customer Experience vision a reality.

_____

_____

_____

b. Train relentlessly. Create a training program and schedule. Every single point of contact with a customer must be examined and tuned: phone calls, interactions in the customer's home or on the sales floor, at the cash register, in-person or telephone complaints, and interactions as the customer leaves...

_____

_____

_____

c. As delivering a great customer experience is a primary objective for your business every year be sure to include that objective into your positive feedback system.

_____

_____

_____

☐
6. Build your customer database. *Do This Now*

   a. Use the most sophisticated tool you can afford, but use something. Consider tools like Microsoft Outlook, Constant Contact (for email & social campaigns), Google Business Apps, your point-of-sale system, or dedicated CRM software like SAP or Salesforce.

   _____

   _____

   _____

b. Record contact information. Contact information should include names, mailing address (especially postal/zip code), telephone number, and email address.

_____

_____

_____

c. Track return business in a way that can be sorted and searched. This is where more sophisticated CRM software starts to pay off.

_____

_____

_____

d. Track referrals. This is also an important part of your customer list: tracking who referred whom. Devise or research a way to track this.

_____

_____

_____

☐
7. Generate that A-List. *Do This Now*
a. Create a list of your best customers using whatever metrics you and your team have selected.

_____

_____

_____

☐

8. Now connect!

a. Say thank you! Set up a schedule and a budget for thanking your top customers and referrers. This can include VIP-only sales and other events; handwritten thank-you notes; special perks...

_____

_____

_____

b. Get personal. Set up a regular schedule for your team to connect with customers in person. This can be by handwritten notes, or personal telephone calls.

_____

_____

_____

c. Set up an email newsletter. Use your POS system, or a dedicated product like Constant Contact or Mail Chimp to send nicely formatted, high-value newsletters to your customers.

☐

9. Get social. After you have set up a CMS system and/or an email newsletter, investigate the roles social networks can play in extending your customer retention reach.

a. Take the time to find a good social media consultant or coach. Ask hard questions about ROI and brand consistency.

_____

_____

_____

b. Explore each social channel separately. Facebook is nothing like Twitter, and LinkedIn and YouTube are different again. Some may be a fit for your business, but not others.

_____

_____

_____

☐

10. Develop a loyalty program. Find some way of rewarding repeat business above new business. Loyalty cards—or any program that provides a discount or a value added extra for consistently loyal customers - are a must.

_____

_____

_____

☐

11. Close the training loop.

a. Now that you have started the process of connecting with, and adding value to your customer relationships, be sure to involve your team every step of the way. Where employees show a talent for this, provide training and use your positive feedback systems to encourage Great Performances.

_____

_____

_____

b. After testing and reporting, record your most effective customer experience boosters in your Standard Operating Procedures manual. Find those things that work, and stick to them.

☐

12. In conversation with your team members, identify the strengths that exist on your team (including your own).

_____

_____

_____

☐

13. Identify any gaps in your team after writing your customer experience charter. #3. Is there anything you must do for your customers, but can't because you don't have the people on your team?

_____

_____

_____

☐

14. Always Be Recruiting
    a. Set a day and time each month to interview for talent.

_____

_____

_____

b. Set up Talent Seeking ads at whatever level you can afford, but certainly include a *Join Us* page on your website, use free sites like Craigslist, Kijiji, and UsedEverywhere, and use social networks to create a 24/365 presence in the world.

_____

_____

_____

c. Develop procedures and policies around posting, screening, and interviewing. Include who should be on your Talent Scout committee.

_____

_____

_____

d. Run your processes and procedures past a human resources specialist in your area to ensure your approaches are consistent with local labour and employment laws.

☐

15. Create A Positive Feedback System

a. Establish regular one-on-one strengths meetings that focus on nothing but how the employee can best connect their strengths to the organizations objectives.

_____

_____

_____

b. List the triggers of your employees. Do they respond well to verbal feedback? Team celebrations? Money? Time off? Tools to help them see how they are doing in competing with themselves (charts, metrics, etc.)?

_____

_____

_____

c. Create checklists to make feedback routine in your operation. How many employees will you check on each week? How much time will you spend on the shop floor? When and how is feedback delivered? What metrics are you using to ensure you are addressing the right objectives in the right way?

_____

_____

_____

d. Write your Positive Feedback System into your HR documentation. How does consistently great performance affect compensation? How will you address consistent under-performers?

♫♫♫

ACT II: Maximizing Limited Resources

Performance Note

Every business on earth has the same three resources:
time, people, and money.

THE CASE STORIES

Band Camp Performance

There was a steady dripping sound coming from Dawn and Rhonda's specialty sporting goods store Xtreme Chances—but it wasn't from the pipes. After three years in operation, it was the sound of time, money, and people leaking from the business.

When the two friends opened the business, it looked like it was going to be a huge success. The store focused on the equipment and culture of skateboarding, BMX biking, and snowboarding in the winter. The location was excellent. In that first year, they earned almost $600,000 in revenues and generated over $100,000 in profits. They sold out of many of their SKUs (Stock Keeping Unit, the retail designation for any item for sale) part way through the season. This was great for inventory, but customers left the store disappointed at the selection more often than the owners liked.

High on the success of that first year, the team invested in more inventory and a full-time manager. Both of the owners kept part-time jobs in other careers because they didn't want to pull too much cash out of Xtreme Chances. The hours they put into their jobs and at the store were exhausting; it put a dent in their social and family lives. So a full-time manager seemed like a logical answer.

Wanting to build on the growth of their first year, the pair invested generously in inventory commitments for the second year. They paid for that with some of the profits from year one, and a mix of personal lines of credit and credit cards to pay for the balance.

On the structural side, things were "a bit sketchy" in Dawn and Rhonda's words. Xtreme Chances was not a limited-liability company (incorporated). There was no written agreement that governed their partnership, but they had been friends since childhood, and they knew they could figure anything out. Rhonda had a home with a mortgage and she already agreed they could borrow against that if they needed to.

As the second year started up, the store looked great: lots of new product lines and SKUs. No one was going to leave Xtreme Chances disappointed at the selection this year!

But year two was surprisingly tougher. Sales fell. The inventory moved more slowly than they had planned, and some of it didn't move at all. The manager they hired, Dave, appeared to be doing a good job and customers really liked him, but turnover of sales staff seemed high. The high-school students and 20-somethings who Dave hired consistently disappointed him. They either left or he let them go.

After disappointing sales in the first two quarters, Dawn and Rhonda increased the advertising budget substantially in anticipation of the snowboarding season. To make up for the increased expenses, both friends took on more hours at their day jobs and drew even less from the store.

The winter season came and went and store profits fell further behind. Few customers who had come in the year before returned. Dawn and Rhonda couldn't be sure because they didn't use their Point-of-Sale system to track anything about their customers. There was never time in those first hectic 18 months! All Dawn and Rhonda knew was store traffic was down, and so were per-customer sales. Customers seemed to love the store, but many of them browsed more than they bought.

As planning for year three began, the two friends were concerned. They were working a lot more at their jobs, with Rhonda working full time. Dave, the manager, spent most of his time on the sales floor because there wasn't enough business to justify a lot of full-time staff.

They did have a huge end-of-season inventory blowout that was successful. Both Dawn and Rhonda spent the weekend at the store for it, and interacted with many of the customers. Again, the feedback about the store was positive, and this time people did buy. In the end though, the steep discounts meant that while inventory moved, there was little money left over to cover operating costs.

Conversations between Dawn and Rhonda became increasingly tense as debt mounted and both friends felt overworked and overwhelmed. Dawn believed the first year had proven there was a market for Xtreme Chances, and the business just needed more time to get off the ground. She asked her friend to take out a loan secured by her home. Rhonda wasn't comfortable and refused.

Year three was a disaster. Sales continued to fall, and even the reduced inventory moved slowly. There was less money for staff and advertising. Dave ran the store by himself and was showing the signs of burn-out. More than once he called in sick and no one was able to replace him. They just closed the store for the day.

When I was called in to see what I could do, it was not a fun conversation. Not only were the partners wrung out, they were in the dark about what happened. Many of the questions I asked them about marketing, customer tracking, or financial tracking and planning were met with "I don't know" or "We've never talked about that."

Dawn and Rhonda were rapidly running out of time and money, and had few people left they could turn to for support. After our meeting, I sent the partners my assessment and recommendations. I never heard back. Twelve months later I did hear the business closed.

♫

Great Performance

After 7 years in business, the team at **NCF (No Casual Fridays)** Design of Victoria, BC opened a second office in Calgary, Alberta. Business was excellent and demand for their services was strong in both provinces. They had a solid client base in 5 cities and spent a lot of their time traveling. Opening an office in their fastest-growing market only made sense.

It wasn't just the sales that drove that decision, however. They hired a designer four years previous; she turned out not only to have great design chops, but was a true rainmaker. She converted contacts, leads, and relationships into customers at a rate the rest of the team could barely keep up with. When they offered her the chance to run her own office in Calgary, she jumped at it.

NCF Design is a graphic and industrial design firm owned by Darrel. Darrel not only loved his industry, he absolutely understood he was running a business. He understood early that anything he put into the business had to show a return or needed a review.

Early in the game, Darrel leveraged employees and a network of contractors and partnerships to get stuff done. Darrel understood there was only so much time, but that lots needed doing. He focused on building and sustaining relationships.

Clients loved him because he always seemed to have time for them, and his employees and partners loved him because he focused on taking care of clients and completing projects rather than micromanaging processes or protecting turf.

NCF Design billings grew quickly. Darrel was careful to reinvest as much of the revenue back into growth as he could. Almost everything he did was based on the budget and growth plan we developed in year four when I started working with him. He leveraged relationships into contra arrangements (exchanging services or products instead of paying for them) rather than pay cash, and monitored cash flow almost obsessively. He knew revenues and profitability would come if he treated people right, and managed his expenses carefully, but cash flow needed daily monitoring so that debt would not become an impediment to growth.

One thing Darrel did early was establish himself as a *premium* designer. His work wasn't cheap, and in the first few years he lost his share of clients as a result.

Another trend also emerged early: a good number of the businesses who first went with one of NCF's cheaper competitors ended up back on Darrel's doorstep a year or two later ready to do business. Over and over again they told stories about how poorly they had been treated by the competition, telling tales of missed deadlines, zero communication, and just a feeling that once the other firm had won their business, their business didn't really matter. No discount could compensate for that kind of treatment.

Darrel was as careful about how he spent his money as how he spent his time. He knew by choosing to bootstrap his growth on a tight budget he would have to put in the hours and rely on the support of everyone in his life. Darrel kept his focus on people. He dedicated enormous amounts of time to clients and designing, and to connecting with everyone who mattered to him and his business. To the outside world it looked like he spent far too much time in coffee shops and shooting the breeze in other people's businesses. The truth was there was not a single person who mattered to the growth of NCF Design including clients, suppliers, top referrers, or other businesses that were NCF Design allies, who did not hear from Darrel at least once a week. Many of those people did not see how many hours Darrel spent working on projects late into the night. *For Darrel, the days were for people, the nights were for getting their work done.*

Darrel had a magical way of squeezing just that little bit more effort out of those around him by making them feel like his success just wasn't possible without them. I know, because when I started working with him, I found myself going out of my way to support him, well beyond the contracted hours! He had a habit of calling or sending me Facebook messages about things that were going on in his business and asking me what I thought. He never failed to let me know how much the feedback, connections, or project support mattered and how much he appreciated it.

He poured his hours into his friends, customers, employees, and supporters, and we poured ourselves into his business.

At the 7-year mark, NCF Designs was cash rich, had no unsecured debts, was seeing annual growth of about 27%, was hugely profitable, opening an office in Calgary, and had a team of 19 and counting.

What was the most fun about having NCF Designs as a client after four years of hard work was there was so much room to play. Finances were excellent, they had a fantastic team, and Darrel never deviated from taking the time required to take care of people and planning. This meant when a decision was required that would grow the business, or add some fun new element to NCF's offerings, the time, money, and people were there to get it done.

As we planned and executed the expansion into Calgary, there were a lot of stressful moments and frustrations. What made it such a Great Performance was the resources were seldom in doubt. The momentum never faltered; no corners were cut. Like everything else Darrel had done in NCF Designs, the Calgary move was the right thing done the right way at the right time.

With Darrel you always had the sense, even after 7 years, things were just getting started.

♫♫♫

Performance Note
"Life is constantly providing us with new funds, new resources, even when we are reduced to immobility. In life's ledger there is no such thing as frozen assets."
Henry Miller

Popsicle Sticks

Every small business has three resources: **time, people, and money.** How you use those resources is what defines a Great Performance.

It is impossible to start and grow a business without these elements, and very difficult to grow without a lot of all three.

When I first meet with a business owner, those resources are among the uppermost things in my mind. I am there to increase the performance of the business, and that requires resources. The question is: *"Do you have the resources, and in what kind of mix, to make a Great Performance possible?"*

Let's get the worst-case scenario out of the way at the start: you have hit a wall and there is nothing left. Your financial resources are tapped out, your line of credit maxed, and you are too shaky a proposition for an equity investor. You and your team are already working 24/7 and there is no money left for more staff. This is a terrible and terrifying position to be in.

There are Great Performances and there is Band Camp, but

sometimes there are shows that just don't go on.

When I talk about the three resources, I often compare them to pry bars or crow bars, to create the image of the leverage they provide. When a business is in the terrible situation I described above, I say the pry bars have been ground down to popsicle sticks. There just isn't much heavy lifting you can do with a popsicle stick.

Unfortunately, when first assessing a business for coaching I do sometimes find a *fatal lack of resources*. There are two things fatal for a business: a failure to connect with a market, and a failure to bring adequate resources to the table.

The hard truth is that sometimes the only option left for me to suggest is a controlled wind-down. This could include selling the business—liquidating what assets the business has, paying off your creditors, and turning off the lights—or bankruptcy.

So much of this book focuses on the positive possibilities and the great resources we have available to us. In business, especially in the world of small business, you simply cannot ignore the dangers and dark sides.

While the rewards of a Great Performance really can be everything you dream they would be, the risks are very large and very real. This is not a world for the faint of heart.

In this section on resources, the first point I want to drive home is: be absolutely clear about the resources available to you before you start your business. Hopes and wishes are not resources. You must have the real thing to grow, or even survive.

With that dire warning out of the way, let's see how you can use resources everyone has available to them to achieve a Great Performance.

♫♫♫

Scene 7: The Resources Of Business

Band Camp Performance:

Running your resources into the ground without even knowing it; making no adjustments or tradeoffs between time, people, and money to leverage the growth of a business.

Great Performance:

Carefully and constantly reviewing your resources and your objectives to see how to get the best high-performance mix; rigorously aligning your resources with what matters most, to get the best possible leverage.

♫

#1: People

Performance Note
The power of people working together
is the only truly magical force in business.

The Only Magic Wand

I am often saying there is no magic wand in business; there are only blood, sweat, tears, time, and money. There just is no pixie dust. This is not entirely true, however. I just don't talk about the one magic wand because I don't want people starting a business with the belief that magical thinking is a substitute for tangible resources. *The one place where magic can happen is with people,* not with time or money.

Why not time or money? Because *time* is the most un-magical of all the resources. It ticks by inexorably and there is nothing you can do to slow it, multiply it, increase it, or bend it...nothing. *Money* is a bit more magical; it can be invested, borrowed, multiplied, shifted around. In the end, at least in the quantities any small business owner can access, those behaviors are linear, logical, and limited. Not much magic there.

People on the other hand, can truly bring a magic-wand moment to a business. That magic is called *creativity*. Unlike time or money, creativity can sometimes make something out of nothing. It can take a dire situation and turn it around. A creative idea truly can save a business *even when the three official resources are tapped out.*

But...

Why not focus more on this? Why not make creativity a fourth resource? Because creativity is notoriously unpredictable. While there are a number of effective ways to increase the chances of having a creative idea, there is *no way* of guaranteeing it.

How many times have we seen in the world of film or music where producers thought buying great talent would guarantee a Great Performance? Remember a film called *Heaven's Gate?* Or *Ishtar?* Tons of high-priced acting talent, and lots of money spent, but they still ended up being a couple of the worst films of all time. No magic there!

The best thing you can do to link creativity to Great Performances is to provide an environment that encourages creativity. Go back to **Act 1** to read the tips on how to do that.

Creativity could be a fourth resource, after time, money, and people. But it is one I would never include in my assessment of the health of a business. It simply cannot be relied upon.

♪

Just Like In The Fairy Tales

Creativity isn't the only unique contribution people can make to the success and growth of a business. Another factor that is also a bit magical is *teamwork*.

Things like teamwork and sacrifice let us be greater than the sum of our parts. *You can't add a 25th hour, but you can ask a team member to stay an extra hour.* You can't, without the intervention of time, make one dollar magically become two, but you can ask a person to bring a friend along to help. Friends, community, and family can sometimes be drawn on as a resource *without tangible cost.* Nothing in life is free—or at least not much. Under certain conditions, true teamwork and the generosity of others can provide a lift without any cost. Sometimes people truly can give freely.

People can be the Shoemaker's elves, the golden harp, the magical beans, or the goose that laid the golden egg. They can transform a business from one state into another without tangible cost, as if by magic.

Flash Point

It should go without saying this is a strategy to use very carefully. Karma, as they say, is a bitch. Draw too much on the Bank of Goodwill, or do so without sufficient gratitude, or too often without recognition and reward, and it will vanish suddenly, unpredictably, and destructively. Just like in the fairy tales! The best advice is to use with caution, gratitude, and without expectations. Then you may see a magical performance.

#2: Time

Performance Note

"Know how to live the time that is given you."
Dario Fo

The Good News

Time is ours. Unlike the other two primary resources, the time we have is ours without question. We can make choices about how to spend that time without getting any from the bank, or asking for anyone's permission.

While people are the most important resource, time is the most powerful. Great Performances require one thing above all else: mastery. *Mastery, skill, practice, and experience.* You, and everyone who is involved in the execution of your business, have to be good at what you do.

In the attainment of that mastery, there is only one element that is absolutely nonnegotiable and necessary. It is not genius, not luck, not birthright or who even we know. It is time.

In his book *Outliers*, Malcom Gladwell famously lays out the 10,000 hour rule he gleaned from the work of people like K. Anders Eriksson and Bill Joy. The book shows us that while privilege, talent, and—very importantly—good luck certainly have a role to play in a great performances, they are not enough. Those things are not why some people achieve greatness. There is only one thing that is the ultimate difference-maker: practice. Ten thousand hours of practice. Practice does not require money (though it helps) and only sometimes requires other people (tough to become a great hockey player alone). In the end, practicing for a Great Performance is simply about putting in the time.

Here is the good news again: time is ours. The time factor for greatness is nonnegotiable, and yet it is the one resource that is free. Yes, the decisions we make to spend our time in one way rather than another do have costs. *But time itself already exists for us.* All of it that we are going to have (though not one second extra) we already have and is freely given. We don't have to earn it or build it up. It is always there for us to use. That is the great gift of all of this: the one thing we need more than anything else is ironically the one thing that we already have. That's pretty cool.

♫

Performance Note
You cannot manage time.
You can only manage priorities.

The Bad News

Everyone thinks money is the biggest challenge in a business: making it, keeping it, growing it. It's not. As I explained above, there is almost always some wriggle room with money. You can borrow some, you can invest it and multiply it; you can delay payments and ask for deposits. Try doing any of that with time.

If you have 10 things you need to do today and despite your best efforts to be efficient, you only get 8 done, there is nothing else you can do. The remaining 2 are going to remain undone until tomorrow. You can't borrow time from someone else and give it back to them later. You can't invest one day's unused hours and get twice as many back a few years later. The day is done.

You Can't Manage It

Time is only conceptually a resource because, unlike money and people, it is impervious to management.

"Wait a minute," you say, "can't you *manage* time? Make choices about how to *spend* it?" No. You can't. "Time management" is a verbal trick that keeps us from focusing on what we really can do. You cannot manage time. You can only manage the way you and your organization behave in the passage of time. You cannot manage time, you can only manage priorities.

The difference in how this language affects our behavior is subtle, but important. I can think of no other reason why people blithely remark, "I don't have time for that," when very clearly the issue is it's just not a priority.

You Can't Spend It

Even when I say you can make choices about how to spend it, the language lulls us into thinking time is a commodity we can control the flow and value of. We can't actually *spend* time. We can only expend our efforts and energy as time flows by as relentlessly as the largest and widest river imaginable.

I make such a big deal about this because our relationship with time is so important, but full of deceptions. Those deceptions creep into the thinking of every manager and business owner sooner or later. You can see it happen as they take on new initiatives, retain control of more processes, broaden the scope of product lines and markets... always *adding, adding, adding.*

You Can't Find It

The first question in a new project should always be: "*Who* is going to do that and *when?*" The next question should be: "What is that person (or team) going to *stop* doing to make that happen?" It never is. The head-in-the-sand approach continues with more verbal sleight of hand: "They will *find* the time." Find it? What, under a seat cushion? In a desk drawer? Lying around in someone else's toolbox unused? There is no finding time! All of it that we have is right here, right now. Do one thing while that hour ticks by, or do something else, but you are not going to find another hour.

The mushy language and subsequent mushy thinking are a barrier to any effort to create a Great Performance. Only a real respect for the value and finite nature of time lets us make the hard choices necessary to being successful.

♫

What You Can Do

Remember Act I? If time is so inflexible and such an impossibly scarce resource, is there anything we can do to improve our odds? Time is inflexible, but can we not get around its rigidity at all?

Yes, we can. There are in particular 3 ways to make a difference in how effectively we use time to achieve Great Performances.

People + Time

Here's a secret to understanding the way to a Great Performance: *resources are tradable.*

Don't have enough time? Invest in people. Grow your team to get done what needs to be done. Want to improve that tradeoff even more? Bring in someone who is better than you at the task and cut the time down even further.

When a business owner tells me they cannot afford a new employee, I know we are in for some educating. You are not looking for an *employee.* In the search for a Great Performance, we are looking for talent, and the definition of superstar talent is *that candidate you can't afford not to hire.*

Great talent always returns more than you invest. Great talent always returns a positive ROI, especially on your investment in time.

Money + Time

Money can also be traded for time. Don't have time? Spend

money. Don't have enough time to get products out, or take care of key process? Buy the equipment or software to automate the process.

The common sentiment notwithstanding, sometimes you can achieve results by throwing money at a problem. It must be done carefully, but it can get results.

Schedules

Performance note
A schedule is your vision mapped against time.

The final tool for getting the very most out of each precious moment is a schedule.

Usually when I bring up the concept of *scheduling* in a conversation with a business owner, you would think I had just dragged my nails across a chalk board. In achieving that Great Performance, schedules are underused and misunderstood power tools.

Schedule Your Vision

Many business owners are big fans of vision boards, affirmations, and journals. These are all tools to create and reinforce a positive vision of our future, whether it is the long-term future represented in a vision board or the shape of a day in morning affirmations.

Schedules are no different. Your schedule is just your vision mapped onto time. Your schedule should show what remarkable things you have planned, and what steps you will take each day to get there.

In creating a Great Performance this is important. As an artist, you would need to book the show, but you also need to commit to rehearsals, talent searches, promoting, and the daily practice of your craft. No one in the performing arts thinks you can just show up on the day of the show and create a Great Performance. In business we tend to think if we just show up each day, without scheduling each step required to get us there, a Great Performance will just materialize. That's not going to happen.

♫

Understanding the possibilities and limitations of the resources a business has is critical to success. Time, people, and money are the resources of any business. Businesses get themselves into trouble because they don't understand how important these resources are, and that these are *all* the resources there are.

It is not until we are honest about what we are working with, and respectful of the challenges and limitations, that Great Performances become possible.

Now let's dig a little bit deeper into the element of time, and how you can approach it to achieve that Great Performance.

#3 Money will be continued in scene 9 because we want to explore it separately.

♫

Journal Intermission

- List three business-related activities someone you know personally could perform more efficiently than you.

- List 3 things that will move your business forward but that require no other resources except time.

♫♫♫

Scene 8: The Three Cycles (More About Time)

Band Camp Performance:

Focusing only on what is most immediately pressing; running in the hamster wheel of sales and delivery.

Great Performance:

Dividing your activities with intention between current operations, monthly and annual growth, and the long-term vision for your business.

♫

The Hamster Wheel

Most small-business owners live a day-to-day or month-to-month existence. As long as the bills are paid, and there is a little money left over at the end of the day, everything is good. That is a band-camp performance. You will never make it to Hollywood or Broadway, or ever sign a recording deal based on a performance like that.

There is no Great Performance without a long game. As a tool to help businesses see there is so much more to the way we unfold our business over time, I have developed a way to divide the time we need to create a Great Performance in business, into three cycles.

In an inspiring article called *The Logistics of Time* , John Jantsch explores the idea that every business has three clocks it must attend to: Real Time, Deal Time, and Meal Time. I owe Jantsch a debt of gratitude for inspiring my own thinking in this.

Jantsch proposed three marketing clocks:

1. Real-time monitoring of the environment.
2. Relationship-building, converting, and closing deals.
3. Building the long-term security of your meal-ticket by focusing on the deeper work of your vision, mission, and values.

Jantsch provides a compelling case for the importance of keeping your long game front and center operationally to build a truly sustainable business. If you are not yet familiar with Jantsch and Duct Tape Marketing, I would strongly suggest you to check out his blog. You will find recommendations and links at the end of this book.

Jantsch's idea arises from the world of sales and marketing. I have taken this strong metaphor and expanded it to describe the management of the whole enterprise.

♬

Every business must function at three levels: the **Current Cycle**, the **Growth Cycle**, and the **Deep Cycle**. I have a lifelong interest in music and acoustics, and I see these three cycles as being like sound waves: high, medium, and low. Check out the end of this Act if you are interested in more detail on this topic.

From a musical performance perspective, you can think of the current cycle as being the melody, the growth cycle as being the harmony, and the deep cycle as being the bass. They all need to work together to achieve a Great Performance in music or in business.

♬

One Turn At A Time

Performance Note
*Failure in the Current Cycle is the failure
to deliver on your marketing promises.*

The Current Cycle

The Current Cycle is about delivering on products and services already sold. The Current Cycle happens after the cash register rings.

This cycle captures the business functions of accounting, operations, logistics, and human resources. There is a great deal of repetitive, predictable, and reactive activity. This cycle isn't sexy, but failure to attend to it, to commit time to its maintenance and tuning, means sure failure. Failure in the Current Cycle is the failure to deliver on your marketing promises.

The turns of the Current Cycle are very short: somewhere between hourly and monthly.

The Growth Cycle

The Growth Cycle captures everything that gets the *next* sale, hires the *next* employee, or plans for the *next* equipment upgrade. In this cycle, the focus areas (pricing, networking, promoting, acquiring, evaluating) typically require more creativity than the current cycle. The rhythms of the growth cycle are not as brisk as the Current Cycle, but are still fairly intense.

The turns of the Growth Cycle are monthly to quarterly.

The Deep Cycle

The Deep Cycle is about the long, slow, deep building that ensures the sustainability of your business *over decades*. The period of the Deep Cycle is between 18 months to 5 or even 10 years.

The lowest note in a musical harmony is called the fundamental. The deep cycle is about building *fundamentals*, building foundations, and planning future directions.

The Deep Cycle may contribute nothing to current revenues, but it is where great leadership makes the greatest impact. The Deep Cycle is about imagining the future: new markets, new services, new methods of delivery, and sometimes entirely new business models.

♫

The Price Of Distraction

Performance Note
When you are looking for a crisis,
everything looks like a crisis.

When a business assigns the right focus and resources to each cycle, it creates a harmony (an idea also introduced by Jantsch). The question is what are the optimum levels of focus and resources required by each cycle?

The answer is nothing new: focus on what is important rather than what is merely pressing. We have a tendency to focus on the squeakiest, the immediately pressing thing, rather than on what makes the difference in our businesses over the long haul.

While taking care of a crisis, particularly one involving your customers or team members, might take priority, the truth is that most business owners overrate the crisis-level of most situations.

Create a schedule for what matters and stick to it. Even when it feels like there are a dozen minor crises all around you. Understand that they may be important, but always consider if they are a) as important as they feel in that moment, and b) if they are more important than the long term health of your business.

The biggest challenge with not being truly committed to scheduling what is important, when you are *looking for a crisis, everything looks like a crisis!* There is no easy solution to those moments. If tending to current crises becomes your daily routine, you will pay a very serious price for that distraction: growth, and the possibility for a long-term Great Performance, will vanish.

♫

Commit To A Schedule

Performance Note
*Either you fill up your agenda, or
crises and squeaky wheels will.*

Committing to a schedule is one of the hardest things to do in business. Everything feels more important or more enjoyable than what we should be doing. The cost is almost nothing that creates the Great Performance gets done.

One sure way to experience everything as a crisis, and constantly run around reacting to external agendas, is to have an empty schedule. To paraphrase a very old saying, *"The devil finds work for an empty schedule."*

Conversely, one of the best ways to keep your environment from setting your agenda, is to set your own.

Here are some ways to structure your hours and years to ensure that your agenda serves your vision, and keeps the Growth- and Deep-Cycle focus required for a Great Performance.

♫

The Current Cycle - Curtains Up

Band Camp Performance:

A restaurant that is able to produce just enough good meals to raise expectations, only to smash them when the customer next comes back and gets a lousy meal.

Great Performance:

A restaurant knocking out memorable meals every day, under any conditions, lunch time or at 11:00 PM, whether the chef is in the house or not.

♫

The Current Cycle consists of the daily and weekly to-do lists, memos, and daily check-ins that provide optimum environments for your employees, and flawless service for your customers. This cycle is about the operations of your business.

The Current Cycle is the performance! Preparation is done, planning has taken place, we have practiced and trained like crazy, we know where we are going. The curtains are now up. Whatever is going to happen, is going to happen. Time to perform; time to execute.

How Much Time Should You Spend At This Level?

Performance Note

"Failure is not a single, cataclysmic event. You don't fail overnight. Instead, failure is a few errors in judgment, repeated every day."
Jim Rohn

How much time you spend on the Current Cycle depends on the quality of the planning done in the longer Growth and Deep Cycles. The more thorough the larger plans, the less the strain on resources in executing your Current Cycle. Great athletes, musicians, and dancers trust the months and years of working on the fundamentals to guide their performances in this moment.

Remember this is not just about executing the Current Cycle work (doing, shipping, producing, etc.) it is the planning of operational work that we are also concerned about.

As a practice, spend about an hour a week and 10 to 15 minutes each day structuring and reviewing short-term plans.

Notes

In the theatre world, every performance day ends in notes. The director, cast, and crew review the performance for required improvements and changes for the next performance.

In better restaurants, every shift begins with an overview of the upcoming bookings, specials, and other directions from management, the kitchen, and the bar.

The idea in each case is that you provide your performers the best and most current information and feedback. You don't allow days or weeks to go by without reviewing performances, or ensuring everyone on your team has the most current information. Without these notes you are allowing small mistakes and false assumptions to slowly drag your show off-course.

In the performing arts world rehearsals and reviews are a daily reality. The world of sports is no different. Great Performances in the business world are impossible without the same commitment to constant practice and ongoing reviews.

While 10 minutes each day is not much time, that is not an indication that it is unimportant. If I see one mistake too many businesses make at the operational level, it is the failure to make daily meetings or notes part of the organization's culture.

Early Warning

Performance Note
Pay now, or pay later;
but you will always pay.

If you find yourself spending more than 110 minutes per week planning and reviewing the daily execution of your business, something may be wrong. It means planning that should have taken place at the Growth- and Deep-Cycle levels may not have. Careful longer term planning and designing has a huge impact on the Current Cycle. Every minute you put into that planning and training work, will save you 10 minutes of reactive crisis management.

10-Minute Focus

Since the Current Cycle largely has to do with the delivery of promises already made, your focus should be operational: efficiency, employee experience, and customer experience.

You will notice most of these things are also *internal* to your business. In the planning and review done in this cycle, you aren't much concerned with the outside environment. The Current Cycle is all about what you are doing *with* your products and services, and *for* your customers and employees when they come into your building.

Current Cycle reviews are not the time to beat things to death. Make a note, keep moving. This is the time for tweaking the details, not for completely rewriting the script, the score, or the choreography.

Can You Tune Your Inputs?

During your planning and reviews ask this question: *can we make even better use of the resources we have to deliver a great customer experience?*

How Is Your Audience Reacting?

This is also the time to review the outputs. Are your products and services the best they can be? From an employee experience perspective, what can be done to improve your workplace?

Play It Sam!

In business there are few things as useless as a one-time wonder. You are *almost* better off to be consistently mediocre than to raise false hopes with unpredictable brilliance, only to disappoint on future deliveries.

When you are consistently mediocre at least you can set your prices accordingly, and your customers will never be disappointed. Sad, but true.

A core focus in your Current Cycle meetings should be consistency. This is the time to point out where small deviations from standard practice resulted in less-than stellar products or service. These small course corrections help prevent big disasters in the future. Regular low-intensity check-ins are central to Current Cycle planning and review, and prevent that slow invisible drift that wrecks so many businesses.

Journal Intermission

- Think back to your most recent complete day in your business. If that day were a play and you were the director, what notes would you give the performers (yourself and your staff)? What went well you want to see more of? What were some mistakes you don't want to see at the next performance?

- Continue to think of your business day as a performance. Write down one thing you or your staff could do that would make your audience gasp in wonder if you did it. Cool gift wrap? A telephone call? Something that requires assembly delivered already assembled? Write it down and do it.

♫♫♫

The Growth Cycle

Performance Note
*"The aim of marketing is to know and understand the customer
so well the product or service fits him and sells itself."*
Peter F. Drucker

Band Camp Performance:

A business owner spending all of his time putting out fires and running in circles, missing opportunities to react to shifts in the market. Products and services remain unchanged for months and even years. There is no marketing, only sales.

Great Performance:

A business owner constantly monitoring her environment to capitalize on shifts and changes by tweaking products and services. There is a constant feedback loop between the market and how the business is marketing.

♫

The Growth Cycle captures those monthly and quarterly plans and activities that lead to the next sale, the next client, the next project. If the industry in question were farming, the growth cycle would be everything about the next planting and harvest cycle.

Marketing is the core of the Growth Cycle. Mid-range financial planning, staffing decisions, and operational changes are also to be looked at. Everything is geared towards performance and growth in the next 1 – 3 years.

How Much Time Should You Spend On The Growth Cycle?

As a practice, spend ½ day each quarter and an hour each month reviewing and structuring your growth plans. That represents about 6 hours per quarter.

As with the Current Cycle, the resources you require to effectively manage the Growth Cycle are determined by how good your long-term (Deep Cycle) planning is. If you have your larger vision and mission clearly set, the Growth Cycle planning work falls into place relatively easily.

You can start to see the pattern: each planning layer has an impact on the smaller layer within it. *Take the time to get the bigger picture right, and you spend less time arm wrestling the details.*

If you are putting together a film or play, and you know what you want the final experience to be, it makes hiring the actors and directors, choosing your locations or sets, clearer. That in turn helps you make good decisions about rehearsal and shooting schedules, or what kind of marketing you are going to do.

A well-planned foundation always makes the next layer easier.

Planning = Meetings

The Growth Cycle should be the main focus of your regular monthly staff meetings.

Scheduling a couple of hours each month, and a half-day each quarter for Growth Cycle work ensures your organization is growing the way you envisioned. Also, effective meetings check past events and future decisions against the long term direction of the business.

A Quick Death Or A Slow One?

The Current Cycle focuses on *internal* adjustments and corrections. The Growth Cycle assesses the external environment and determines near-term opportunities. Ironically, while the look outwards is as important as the look inward, most business owners simply don't give it the same focus.

While failing to deliver on your promises will kill you quickly, failing to anticipate where the world and your customers are going next will kill you just as surely, albeit more slowly.

A Great Performance requires a business owner to be a bit like Janus, the Roman god of transitions and doorways. In Roman sculptures, Janus was always depicted as having two faces: one facing forward and one facing back. A successful business owner must have her eyes both on the promises made in the past, and on the possibilities of the future.

An easy example is a restaurant business. Preparing low-quality meals and providing poor service (Current Cycle concerns) will shut you down quickly. Failing to notice your market is shifting towards a gluten-free diet, or demanding a more ethnic flair in their experience, will shut you down more slowly, but will shut you down nonetheless as people slowly drift away.

The market and the business environment never hold still. The economy changes, competitors come and go, your customers' tastes change. To successfully capitalize or respond to any of these environmental changes requires that you detect them as early as possible.

The biggest difference between a band camp performance and a Great Performance in this area is the extent to which the owner has his head down, working in the business alone; or his head up, watching for the inevitable changes the world will throw at his business.

♫

What Am I Doing Here?

Performance Note

*A Great Performance requires harmony between what
the market wants, and what you are delivering.*

As you have seen, the Growth Cycle is about the market, your customers, and the general external business environment. To hear it musically, the Growth Cycle plays the *harmony* role to the Current Cycle's melody, and the Deep Cycle's bass line.

The Growth Cycle creates harmony between where the external environment is heading, and what your business is doing internally to respond. To achieve that harmony requires being *tuned in* to the details in the external environment. Your performance will only be as good as your knowledge of your audience (the market). You have to listen, watch, respond, and often lead.

Always keep in mind a true performance is not some event that happens in isolation. You need an audience. Going through the performance of a ballet, play, or musical number without an audience is a rehearsal. We are not after *Great Rehearsals*; we are after Great Performances.

The same is true in business. A Great Performance is ultimately defined by the market and your customers. The core of all your planning at the Growth Cycle level is defined not so much by your performance as by your ability to listen, watch, learn, connect, respond, and engage.

Listen

Use every tool at your disposal to monitor your environment. Use social media and surveys. Ask your employees and suppliers what is going on out there. Stay current by reading key blogs and following LinkedIn groups relevant to your industry. Bring real data and stories to your meetings.

Of all the things your review and planning in the Growth Cycle must do, keeping your customers close and really seeing them as partners in your growth and plans is most important. Remember retention and relationships are the magic ingredient in great marketing strategies.

Use All Ears

Everyone on your team should know when those monthly and quarterly Growth Cycle meetings happen, they should come loaded with stories and numbers about *what is going on out there.*

Monitoring the environment and having a clear read on what your customers feel and say about you is everyone's responsibility, not just yours or the marketing department's.

Balance Consistency And Flexibility

If the Current Cycle is all about consistency, the growth cycle is all about *measured* changes. Things can be changed, but not without excellent evidence is it the right thing to do.

By the same token nothing is ever retained just because *"that's the way we always do it."* The market is unimpressed by your faithfulness to traditions. Even your customers, while they may love you for brand qualities like being homey or traditional, could drop you in an instant when their nostalgia finds a new flavour, or someone else finds a new way to deliver the same qualities with new twists.

If circumstances demand it, you must be ready to show up in a new way at the drop of a hat.

Lead

Not every decision made in your Growth Cycle planning sessions has to be reactive; in fact, you have to be careful to whom you are reacting.

To react to your customers' changing needs and tastes is one thing, to change because your competitors are, or because your suppliers are pushing you to, is another thing. At all times keep your eyes on who matters most: your own team and your customers.

Sometimes we can even go further.

Steve Jobs of Apple was famous for saying customers did not always know what they wanted. All change driven by the market, or tribal, or community level will be evolutionary. We want things the same as before, only better. Collectively, we are not able to imagine that which doesn't exist yet, like an iPod or an iPad. That kind of change is revolutionary and requires leadership.

There are times when we are looking ahead in the Growth and Deep cycles that we should listen, but not necessarily react. Initiative and leadership are risky, but sometimes you have to risk changing the game yourself.

In marketing we have the concept of a *disruptive* strategy, where a product, service, or story is introduced into the marketplace that completely sets it on its ear. Sometimes when there is no *white space* (opportunities to do something totally new) left in the market, small little adjustments are simply no longer effective.

It is time to risk a disruptive approach.

Take the mouse and the keyboard away from the computer.

Make it neither a smart phone nor a computer, so you can't call people on it, or do office work on it, and provide only one form of input: a touch screen. You risk failing spectacularly if you misjudge your timing or your audience, but you might put together something called an iPad and the performance of a lifetime if you get it right.

♫

Journal Intermission

- Think about the world that surrounds you. Write down three things that are happening in the world that could impact your business, negatively or positively.

- List 3 – 4 ways you could find out about what is going on in the world, or in your industry to help you become a better monitor of your environment. Consider people, the internet, journals, newspapers, etc.

- Practice lateral creativity. One way to do this is to take unrelated things (things that are lateral to what you do, from left field) and bring them into your thinking. Here is an example: how would a homemaker, a baker, and an airline pilot use your product or service? What creative, disruptive, changes would you make to your products or services to make them useful to these three groups?

♫♫♫

The Deep Cycle

Performance Note
"Begin with the end in Mind"
Stephen Covey

Band Camp Performance:

plodding through the years assuming as long as you take care of business every day, the ending will take care of itself; slowly fading into invisibility and irrelevance as the world around you moves on.

Great Performance:

designing your ending at the beginning: knowing if you will be selling, franchising, licensing, or shooting the whole damn thing out of a cannon when you're done; having a business that remains profitable and relevant until the day you decide it isn't.

Deep Cycle work focuses on the long-term future. The time frame is between 18 to 36 months, and can be as far out as 5 to 10 years.

The Deep Cycle is all about dreaming, visioning, strategizing and planning.

Long-Term Planning

Long-term planning is an important exercise in plotting evolutionary change. It is based on one initial question: *"To continue our string of Great Performances, can we build on what we have done and carry on in the direction we have already set?"* If the answer is yes, you are engaged in long-term planning.

At its root, this becomes an exercise in scaling: taking what you already have, and doing more of it. You look at your Current- and Growth- Cycle activities and you expand them into new markets, larger centers, adding more lines of production, considering what variations on existing SKUs, products, and services your market would embrace.

Strategic Planning

In business as in the performing arts, there are times to create new work, and times to recreate yourself. Artists from Beethoven to Madonna to Picasso have had periods or phases in their work. These transformations are not always accidental or evolutionary. Often they are deliberate redesigns and restructuring of the artist's whole process.

These are the disruptive strategies discussed under the Growth Cycle, but applied to the business and the brand itself. These are deep, deliberate, *disruptive* strategic changes. You know you are in a strategic planning process when the answer to the question *"Can we carry on in the same direction, only bigger?"* is "No. It is time to create a new direction."

To quote the title of an excellent book by Marshall Goldsmith, "What got you here, won't get you there."

- You are no longer just scaling up what you already have.
- The audience is drying up, and it is time to come up with a new show altogether.
- If you are IBM you realize your future as a PC-hardware manufacturer is limited.

Time for a new show.

The best book I have read on the imperative for strategic change is Daniel Pink's "*A Whole New Mind*". In his book, Pink suggests we ask ourselves 3 questions about our current or planned endeavours:

114

1. Can a computer do it faster?
2. Is what I'm offering in demand in an age of abundance?
3. Can someone overseas do it cheaper?

If the answer is yes to any of these questions, it is probably time to consider a strategic change.

♬

Why Worry About The Future?

Either you will design your business for the future, or the future will happen to you. A view to the horizon matters whether you are doing basic long-term planning, or more complex strategic planning.

- Bob Dylan picked up an electric guitar.
- Jackson Pollock changed from treating painting as a noun to treating it as a verb.
- IBM changed from a hardware manufacturer into a knowledge business.

Each took control of their worlds. Each engaged in strategic change.

This is the place to decide not *what* you will do next, but *who* you will be next. In the 1.5 to 10 years the Deep Cycle describes, you may decide to continue on as you did before, or you will be someone or something completely different. The critical thing is to decide, rather than letting market forces and the environment decide for you.

In business the designs and plans of the Deep Cycle are worked out in the brand, vision, and mission statements. This is the cycle of rebranding, exit strategies, and succession plans.

Your environment will change as surely as the sun rises and

sets. You must respond to and even anticipate that change, or risk becoming irrelevant as the world changes around you.

It's Rocket Science

One of the rules of planning is the better your foundational planning, the fewer resources (like time) are required to keep the enterprise on track.

Earlier I described how good planning at Deep Cycle level makes Growth Cycle work easier, and good planning at that level makes Current Cycle work easier.

My favourite analogy to illustrate this comes from the science of rocket flight. I know, I know, they say, "This isn't rocket science," yet here we go anyway! When a rocket is launched, there are two ways to ensure it arrives where you want it to: at launch time or through later corrections. If you can set the direction of the initial launch perfectly, you can devote resources entirely to forward motion. This would be the most efficient use of resources. If you get it wrong, and have to course correct along the way, the energy costs are enormous. The rocket may still arrive on target, but you are going to pay.

You can always proceed with the attitude "we'll figure it out as we go along" and there are times when that is appropriate and even necessary. Just be aware the risks of expending precious resources are huge.

Of the resources you have, the loss of time is the most critical. Every hour, day, or year you spend changing or correcting your course is time forever lost to pure forward motion.

The impact on your performance in planning and executing your Current and Growth Cycles is also serious:

- How can you commit to great customer experience and great systems if you are constantly changing direction?
- How can you deliver Great Performances in growing your

fan base and building great relationships if those fans and supporters can't figure out where you are going?

Time To Commit To Deep Cycle Work

Deep Cycle planning is the stuff of annual weekend or day-long retreats and strategic planning sessions. I suggest to my clients that they devote at *least* one full day per year developing long-term strategic plans, and an hour per quarter reviewing and adjusting. So what do we do on these retreats and reviews?

Performance Note

*"Your brand is what people say about you
when you are not in the room."*

Jeff Bezos

Manage Your Brand

Branding is not just for Starbucks and McDonalds. The reality is that everyone has a brand. Your brand is the sum of everything your market thinks about you.

To make sure your brand is doing its part in your Great Performance, take time regularly to review where you want your brand to be in three years, and to ensure you are taking the steps to get there. If you don't, time, the market, and your competitors will make those decisions for you. Trust me, none of those forces is kind or fair.

Branding, and planning for the long-term evolution of your business, is not just for the big guys. A clear brand is for anyone who plans on being the last one standing. Here's how you do that planning.

Deep Cycle Brand Management

Take these 6 steps to envision, design, and control your brand for a great performance.

Performance Note

*Business is nothing less than a social
solution of individual needs.*

1. **Be clear about what your customers most need from you.** The heart of business is solving someone's problem for consideration. To paraphrase the great Harvard marketing professor Theodore Levitt, people don't want a 1/4-inch drill, they want a 1/4-inch hole, and they will pay you for any solution to that problem that works for them. If you can clearly define what one need you serve better than anyone else, you have the heart of your brand.

2. **Understand your customer's journey.** Not only should you know what your customers want right now, you need to know where your customers are going next. This means becoming intimate with the trends, patterns, influences, values, and desires of your market on every level. Great brands never trail their customers; they are right beside them every moment, or even in the lead. In the performing arts, great musicians, playwrights, and film makers create culture as much as they reflect it. Steve Jobs and Apple understood this very well.

Performance Note

*"I would say that listening to the other person's emotions may be the
most important thing I've learned in twenty years of business."*
Heath Herber

3. **Engage**. As in almost everything else in life, we learn much of what really matters in conversation. Learn to ask the right questions, and learn how to listen for the answers, including the answers in the spaces between the words. Can you hear that which is not spoken but felt? Constantly find opportunities to have conversations, both in the face-to-face world, and in the online social world.

4. **Strive for *internal* consistency**. What your customers most value, your employees should value as well. Whatever your central message to your customers, it must be consistent with the one you give your employees. The values, language, and design of your brand should appear like a *leitmotif* (a theme that constantly re-appears in a long piece of music) everywhere your business has a presence. From values to colours; from language to pricing… the whole enterprise must have a deep sense of internal consistency.

5. **Use social media.** It is in the slow work of brand development where social networks really come into their own. The ability to engage your customers and fans, to tell your story, and shape your message through Tweets, Facebook posts, and blog articles puts the communications edge into the hands of small-business owners in a way that was not possible even a decade ago.

6. **Record and share your story.** The social brand of the 21st century is not just about colours, fonts, logos, or slogans any more. Those things still have a role, but they stand almost as ornaments to what really matters: relationships and stories. Using images, language, people, conflicts, challenges, and victories, businesses now have the opportunity to build relationships that can go much deeper than ever before.

This requires paying attention to the moments when things happen, and recording images, events, and words to weave into stories. Just like a candidate for a job can fake it through an interview, any business can fake authenticity for one commercial, but you can't sustain it for the thousands of hours of image, video, and text our customers and fans can now follow and interact with.

Journal Intermission

- List 2 - 3 ways your business solves customers' problems or improves their lives. Now think 3 years down the road. Will those problems still exist? If so, will they have changed in any way?

- Consider one question you would ask a loyal customer about their future that would have an impact on your business.

- Think back over the past year. Is there any image or story that captures the business you would like to become? Did you move into a new market? Did an employee do something remarkable in the business or community? If there is a photo or image that captures the business you are working to become, what is it?

♫♫♫

Great Performances

Scene 9: Money Makes The World Go 'Round!

Performance Note

"A mark, a yen, a buck, or a pound/ A buck or a pound/ A buck or a pound / Is all that makes the world go around/ That clinking clanking sound/ Can make the world go 'round'.

Cabaret

The third and final resource you require for a Great Performance is money.

I left money to last for one simple reason: while it is the resource most people think of *first* when it comes to business, of *People, Time, or Money*, money is the least critical of the three.

Don't get me wrong, money matters, but if you *had* to start a business without one of the three main resources, it would have to be money. Without *time*, you can do nothing. Without *people* (customers if no one else), you can do nothing, but it is *possible* to start a business without money.

Furthermore, money can be borrowed, saved, invested, spent, retrieved, and stolen. None of which you can do with time or people. That fluidity, that accommodating nature money has, means while it matters a lot, it is almost always easier to manage than time.

Point Of View

That said, there is a lot to understand about the financial management of a business. Not only are there many different elements such as income, cash flow, direct and fixed costs, dozens of key ratios, debt, assets, depreciation, amortization, accounts payable and receivable, the financial elements of inventory control and so on, there are also different ways of looking at the whole picture.

In literature and in film there is a very important storytelling tool called *point of view* (POV). POV describes through whose eyes you are seeing events unfold.

In Alfred Hitchcock's brilliant 1954 movie *Rear Window*, we watch as the main character Jeffries (played by Jimmy Stewart), learns things about his neighbours by watching them through the rear window of his apartment. What makes this a masterpiece study in POV is that Hitchcock has his main character confined to his apartment, in a wheelchair. For the better part of the first act, our entire understanding of what is going on is limited to what Jeffries can see from his apartment window. The camera shows us only what he can see. He can't move and neither can we.

Your accountant, investors, and lenders will generally look at the financial elements of a business from one *point of view*. That POV can best be described as being a *value and accrual* perspective. This means those professionals, while considering all reports and statements, use the balance sheet of the business as their primary lens. They are looking mostly at the long-term and annual health of your business.

Your suppliers, customers, employees, you as the owner, and I as your coach will have a different POV. That point of view is a *cash* perspective. The main documents we are concerned with are the income statement and statement of cash flows. We are primarily concerned with monthly changes in revenues and expenses.

Both points of view are critical to the financial health of a business. Both points of view also need to be understood by a business owner to make a Great Performance possible. In my work with small businesses, it is useful (if oversimplified) to understand the owner and I look at their business largely from a cash perspective on the daily, monthly, and even quarterly basis. Yet, at the end of the year, and as it approaches the end of your time as the owner of the business, together with the accountant, we look at the business primarily from the perspective of the balance sheet.

That is not to say that considerations like changes in assets and liabilities don't matter day-to-day, or that sales revenues don't matter when it comes time to exit your business. They do, tremendously, but it is a question of focus.

We clearly have a lot to explore here, so let's get started.

* Flash Point *

The usual caveat applies: "Do not try this at home." This Scene lays out the financial big picture in broad strokes for small-business owners seeking to master the cash fundamentals of their business and those trying to understand the financial implications of debt and exits/succession. This is no substitute for a good accountant who is willing to sit down with you regularly and review the financial health of your business!

♫

A Play

In the spirit of our performing arts theme, let me present a brief scene, played two ways.

A Financial Band Camp Performance

Me [to Business Owner]: *"Tell me a bit about your financial situation."*

Business Owner: *"We are doing great! We made 1.2 million at the end of last year, and this year we are looking to increase that by adding two more machines. There never seems to be any money in the bank at the end of the month, but I know we're OK because we always seem to pay our bills on time!"*

A Financial Great Performance

Me: *"Tell me a bit about your financial situation."*

Business Owner: *"We are doing OK. Our year-end saw about $180,000 in profits before paying ourselves, on about $1.2 million in gross revenues. We paid ourselves $120,000. Our direct costs are under control, but we have some questions about fixed operating costs because they increased by 14%, but then our sales revenues only increased by 12%. We are still profitable, but are wondering if that is a warning sign. Cash flow is an issue because some of our accounts don't pay for 60 or even 90 days. We need to increase production, but the cost of financing two new machines is going to hurt cash flow even more."*

In the band camp performance, all the owner could tell me about was sales revenue. He is talking about expanding, but is focusing entirely on doing that by expanding capacity. He assumes there will be money coming in the cash register if he just makes more stuff. He has no idea what goes out as expenses, except the bills seem to be getting paid.

In the answer of the great performer I hear someone who knows that managing the finances of a business is a complex, layered reality. She is aware of the relationship between sales revenues, and the different kinds of costs (direct, variable or fixed). She also gets there is a difference between profit and what an owner puts in her jeans at the end of the day. She touches on the fact that you can be profitable at the end of the year, and still feel the impact of poor cash flow each month. Finally, she sees that growth is about more than just buying new equipment or hiring new employees. She knows the cost of growth must always be accounted for.

The Revenues, Profit, & Cash Flow Triangle

Of all the financial mistakes I see small-business owners make, the most common is focusing exclusively on revenues.

Revenues are only one part of the picture, and a deceptive part at that. Businesses can get themselves into serious financial trouble because they only see the money coming in. As long as the number is big and growing, they are lulled into thinking everything is OK.

The truth is that from the cash POV, there are 3 elements you must be in command of to achieve a Great Performance: revenues, profit, and cash flow.

Revenues

Revenue, or the money you take in at the cash register, is the simplest to understand. Ironically, it is most like the weather: something you don't have a whole lot of control over. Revenues are the consequence of other things you do in your business: the quality of your products or services; the quality of the customer experience, your marketing and advertising strategies (including pricing); and the quality of your employees.

Revenues are simple because the only math required is counting. Revenues are challenging because to increase your revenues is a complex and slow process that has very little to do with money and everything to do with your products and services.

Profit

Profit is more complex than revenue, but not by much. At its most basic, your profit is the consequence of your revenues less all the expenses that go into running your business. That is where things stop being simple.

For one thing, there is more than one kind of profit. You

can have gross profit, which is the profit from one particular product or service after deducting the costs directly associated with making or providing that product or service. Then you have net profit, which is the profit after deducting *all* the costs not directly associated with producing that product or service: things like rent, heat, most labour costs, advertising, etc.

The complications don't stop there. Once you have all your expenses accounted for, how will you handle the profits? When and how do you pay yourself? The answer to that may be different depending on whether you are talking to the tax people, to your accountant, or me. Depending on the country you live in, and the way your business is set up, you could pay yourself as an employee receiving wages; you could be a shareholder who is paid in dividends; or it could be a mix of the two. Your income may show up on the business's income statement, or it might not. Then there's the money that flows in and out of your shareholder loan. This is why a good bookkeeper and an accountant are so important to the success of your business.

Cash Flow

Cash flow is the measure of a business's ability to pay its bills at the end of each month. A positive cash flow means that at the end of the month you had enough money to pay all the bills and accounts payable due that month. Negative cash flow means you either failed to pay your bills on time or you had to go into debt (often a line of credit) to pay them.

Cash flow is impacted not just by whether your income is greater or less than your expenses, it is also impacted by timing. Cash flow is impacted by *when* the money comes in and when the bills are due.

If your sales revenues were $10,000 this month, and your total expenses are only $6,000 then you should be in good shape, right? You have netted 40% profit! Happy dance, right?

Not so fast. What if the supplies you used to create the products or support the services are all on invoices payable at the end of the month? What if your customers don't all pay for 30 days? Or 45? Or 60? What if some of those supplies are cash only? What if you have to pay cash right now to make a product you might not sell for a month or two? *That* is the dilemma of cash flow.

♫♫♫

Fitting It All Together

Performance Note
Money is the sound of business.

The *foundation* of a Great Performance in business is people. The *measure* of that performance in business is money.

In the performance of music you need *people*: musicians and audience members. The currency of that performance, what flows back and forth between the people, is *sound.*

Money is the sound of business. Money is the measure, the currency of the relationship a business sets up. To achieve that Great Performance you must have complete control over that currency. That is the sound of success.

Revenues, profit, and cash flow form the basic triangle on which a Great Performance is built. As with any triangle, there are a number of ways the sides and angles can relate to each other. Let's have a look at the ones that matter in business.

♫

Managing Revenues & Profit

As we described earlier, profit at its simplest is what is left over after you have deducted your expenses from your revenues. It stands to reason that if it is difficult to have much control over your revenues, the important variable is the control of your costs. You must control your costs on two levels: direct (or variable) costs, and fixed costs.

Your direct or variable costs, often called the cost of goods sold (COGS), are directly associated with the cost of each product or service you provide, and they vary as the numbers of products do. If your direct cost to produce a cupcake is $1, then ignoring the economies of scale for the moment, 10 cupcakes should cost you $10.

Your fixed costs are so called because they are fixed. Whether you produce and sell 100 cupcakes or 1000, your fixed costs remain the same. You still have to pay heating bills, administrative costs, rent, advertising costs, and so on. Those are fixed costs.

So your poor beautiful sales revenues get squeezed twice! First they have to pay the dance partner that brought them (direct costs), and then they have to pay the orchestra (fixed costs)! And the orchestra must be paid even if your products or services never got a single dance!

To convert all of those good revenues into better profits, it is the expenses that need managing. Increasing revenues alone does not always increase profit. Reducing expenses almost always increases profit. Here is your list of Great Performance tips to build those profit margins.

Watch For Secretarial Spread

Not the Weight Watcher's kind, the overpopulation kind. As a small business, if you are *forced* to choose between reducing your direct costs or your fixed expenses, the latter is often your better choice.

Why? Because your direct costs are closely associated with the quality of product you are producing. As a painter, sure you can go for a cheaper brand or line of paint, but either you are going to have to put more coats on the walls or produce a lower quality finish for your customer. Neither is a great option. You want to control costs as far from your primary products or services as possible.

Having a great administrative support team, or a good advertising campaign, are very important to your business. If you are forced to choose between them and quality inputs for your products, fixed cost items like administration and management must receive the closer scrutiny.

Sometimes Size Matters

There is a great deal of suspicion out there about growth. It has almost become a dirty word because of the uncontrolled expansion of multinational corporations. Getting bigger can have powerful positive impacts on small businesses.

When you are bigger you have more ability to control your direct costs, not something that is otherwise very easy to do. When you are bigger you can buy in bulk. You can buy supplies in ever-larger quantities and take advantage of the *discounts* that bulk buying usually comes with. On the side of your revenues, size can also matter. While we try to control our direct or variable costs as much as possible, the bottom line is some businesses are very expensive and the margins very small, so the only way to increase profits measured in dollars (rather than percentages), is to get bigger.

I have clients where some costs, like fuel, are simply not negotiable, so they can't shrink that direct cost, and they can only shrink their administrative costs so far. The pain of reducing those costs by one more percentage are simply not worth it because there are unintended costs created elsewhere (as in employee turnover). There is often only one answer in these cases: go big. How does this work?

Let's say that cupcake business we met earlier has fixed costs (rent, utilities, administration, etc.) of $1000 per month. They make cupcakes that they sell for $6 and cost $5 in direct costs, or COGS, to make. At a $1 gross profit per cupcake you would have to make and sell 1000 cupcakes just to break even (cover your direct and fixed costs) in this oversimplified example.

Now, if they could make 1100 cupcakes would they have to hire more administrative personnel? Heat more of the building? Advertise more? Probably not. How about 1200 or 1500 or 2000 cupcakes? Maybe.

The bottom line is many businesses can increase their level of products manufactured or sold, or services delivered, without increasing their fixed costs. That is where getting bigger can be profitable. Calculating how much more you can produce before your fixed costs do start to go up is beyond the scope of this book. How many cupcakes can you make and sell before you have to increase the size of your production facility, or increase your labour costs, or administrative costs?

If you want to start your own exploration of that, look up terms like marginal cost, economies of scale, and capacity utilization.

Micromanage Here!

Micromanagement has a bad name, but there are at least two places where micromanagement is *exactly* what's wanted. One is in the training of your staff and their interactions with customers, and the other is on the planning and tracking of your finances.

Particularly if your business has more than one revenue source, whether that is different sales people, different SKUs, or different activities altogether (a gardening business that has both retail sales and a landscaping service), it is critical you micromanage the performance of each one. You must know which of your activities are profitable, and by how much. Each activity your business is involved in must not only pay for itself (gross profit), but must also show that it can carry its share of the operating expenses or fixed costs of your whole business.

No one rides for free.

♫

Managing Revenues and Cash Flow:

Timing Is Everything

When it comes to managing cash flow in an otherwise healthy business (your revenues are sufficient and you are profitable), the big challenge is timing.

To manage your cash flows, you must develop a document called a pro forma statement of cash flows. The pro forma statement of cash flows is basically a budget in which you predict the ebb and flow of your business, both on the revenue side and *everything* on the expense side, not just what appears on your income statement. In this budget you project how much each of your activities or products will sell for, when that cash actually shows up in your business, what the direct costs are, and what the fixed-operating costs are. Then you subtract *everything* else, like owner's draws (in any form), financing payments, etc. And you do this for every month of the year.

A cash-flow budget predicts when cash *actually* goes out and comes in. One example of how important it is to know this information is in direct costs. Often the costs you require to manufacture or put an item into inventory must be spent *before you can actually sell it*. If that is the case, you must budget for where the money will come from until the sale actually happens.

The formula is (simplified): Revenues – minus Direct Costs – minus Operating Costs – minus Every Other Damn Cash Outlay! No fancy accounting where you get to hide stuff. *Everything* is counted.

Here is a classic scenario: a seasonal business has strong spring and summer months but weak fall and winter seasons. Averaged over the whole year, the business projects a profit. What happens if there is not enough cash on hand to purchase new supplies at the end of the weak winter to stock inventory for the anticipated strong summer? You can't earn new revenues if you can't purchase inventory. Will you borrow money from the bank? Go into your line of credit? Are you factoring in the cost of that borrowing (interest and principal payments) into your cash budget? Or could you keep a tighter control of your expenses during good times to ensure there is a cash reserve to start the next cycle?

There are many ways to address this classic challenge, but whichever option you choose, you must create a pro forma budget describing where every penny will go. I see where the failure to do that goes every time: debt mounts because its repayment is never truly factored into the budget each year. As debt payments grow, they eat up a business's cash making it even harder to finance new inventory or growth. So then the owner goes even deeper into debt. That cycle never ends well.

♬

Managing Profit & Cash Flow:

Profit Isn't Everything

One of the tricks every great performer in business knows is sometimes lower profits today are better than higher profits tomorrow. Think of it like a blood transfusion: getting the best transfusion in the world in 6 months isn't worth much if you need it today—and every business needs cash today.

If the choice is between cash up front at a lower profit margin, and cash down the road at a higher profit margin, the better choice is often the former. For one thing, poor cash flow will damage your business more quickly than poor profits. If you are not particularly profitable you can limp along for months and even years. Trust me, many businesses do! If your cash flow sucks, you are in trouble at the end of the month. You can't pay your bills, and a *sustained* negative cash flow means that you are not profitable anyway.

So if you are forced to choose, positive current cash flow often trumps long-term higher profits. To keep the cash flowing, it is sometimes worth trading higher margins for quicker payment.

This can be done two ways:

- First, create interest penalties for late payment (usually anything past 30 days).
- Second, reward early payment (such as large deposits or full cash payments on delivery). You can add a marketing twist to the process by charging a premium price for people who pay later and the real price for people who pay early, but call it a discount. I have seen this work very effectively.

Subscribe Here

You can also reward *regular* payment. That is what subscriptions are all about. In exchange for making an automatic regular payment over a longer time period, you can provide the product or service at a discount.

A note here: subscriptions are different from deferred or amortized payments. In a subscription program, the customer signs up for a repeat service or product (like a magazine subscription). In a payment plan, you purchase something once, but pay for it over time. Deferred or amortized payments do not qualify for discounting because they have a negative impact on cash flow. Instead of receiving the full payment for the one product or service, you grant the customer the right to pay you for it over time. You are carrying *their* debt to you and helping out with their cash flow! That is not worth a discount, it is worth a premium.

Subscriptions are powerful because they not only support good cash flow, they are also a tool for retaining customers. That is the reason magazine subscriptions are always so much less expensive than buying one at the store. The publisher knows a subscription means you are theirs for the next 1 - 3 years, requiring no further advertising costs to bring you in, and giving them an opportunity to mail you all kinds of goodies and promotions. Not only do they have your money, they have your mailing address as well.

I am a fan of anything that is structured as a subscription. The benefits to the business on the cash-flow side, and for customer-retention opportunities, are such that it is worth enticing the customer to participate at a discount. You are able to lock in a customer and generate a steady cash stream in ways few other things in business can.

Have a good look at your business. Is there anything you can do to create subscriptions? I have seen landscaping companies offer monthly maintenance and clean-up services, and wineries offer case-of-the-month specials. Training programs, in which you pay a lower monthly fee in exchange for signing a contract to participate for a fixed number of months, are a form of subscription. Each can be very effective.

Turnaround Is Fair Play

Of course, the reverse is true as well: if you have a good cash-flow budget, you know whether your own purchases (inventory, equipment, supplies) should be handled with a single-cash outlay, or financed over time. This is the expense side of the profit versus cash flow tradeoff.

Even with the cost of financing, it is sometimes better to be good to your cash flow and spread out payments over time. There are many out there who avoid financing at all costs because of the interest expense, but that is a narrow view. If it is a difference between using financing to acquire what you need to supply and grow your business, or foregoing growth, or keeping inventory tight, the savings are a false economy.

Journal Intermission

- Which financial area is your business's strong point: revenues (strong sales), profit (good margins), or cash flow (bills always paid, little use of things like lines of credit/overdraft/credit cards to pay suppliers)? Jot down why you believe you are successful in that area, and a couple of things you could do to strengthen the others.

- Do you provide any products or services on a subscription/plan basis? If not consider the products and services you offer. Could any of them be packaged and priced in a way to allow customers to receive them on a monthly basis?

- List your top 10 fixed expenses. If you reduced each of them by 10% what would the impact on your business be?

♫♫♫

Scene 10: Managing Debt

Performance Note

"There are but two ways of paying debt: Increase of industry in raising income, increase of thrift in laying out."
Thomas Carlyle

Band Camp Performance:

Letting debt control your business; sticking your head in the sand while you use debt to bridge negative cash flow; or refusing to get into debt because you are afraid of it.

Great Performance:

Understanding that debt is a powerful tool. Like any powerful tool you have to use it carefully or it can do a lot of damage. You use debt as a lever to grow your business.

♫

Debt Management: The Secret Is Complete Control

If there was one thing I could wish for every one of my clients it is that they live without unmanaged debt.

I have given debt its own section because so many small-business books don't address it, yet *I have seen it crush far more small businesses than poor marketing or negative human resources practices.*

Small business debt is a big deal, and a Great Performance is impossible without addressing it.

The Down Side

As businesses, things become problematic when we let debt compensate for sustained insufficient cash flow. At the personal level problems arise when we let debt support a lifestyle at odds with our real incomes. In both cases, it is the interest servicing that intrudes like a corrosive toxin, further degrading cash flow and ballooning expenses, and eventually becoming part of the very problem it was brought in to solve.

Debt has a role as a powerful lever in bridging transitions or fueling growth, but using it as a mask for poor cash flow and poor choices in life is almost always disastrous.

The Up Side

There are times when debt can play a role in helping you get through a temporary rough patch. But as with managing cash flow, it must be part of a plan.

The plan requires three key parts:

1. **A specific target.** Before you borrow the money, be sure you know exactly where it is going to be spent and how that expenditure will help you increase profitability.
2. **A clear budget.** No debt is free. Even a theoretically interest-free loan will require that you work out the repayment of the principal in a way that doesn't choke your cash flow each month.
3. **A specific time frame.** Your budget should set out exactly how long you expect to repay the debt. If you are unable to repay the debt in that timeframe, that should set alarm bells ringing. This could be an early sign that your business is not being managed well, or that the market for your products is not what you need it to be.

♫

Long-Term Commitment

Performance Note
*"A hundred wagon loads of thoughts
will not pay a single ounce of debt."*
Italian Proverb

Any debt (but especially significant long-term debt) has an impact on your business. Lenders and investors will want to know how much debt you are carrying relative to your ability to repay that debt. If they see that the size of the debt is growing while your ability to service that debt is not, it will set off alarms. On a more subtle level, if there is a trend that you are increasingly relying on debt to finance your business, rather than on your equity (as measured in your debt-to-equity ratio), that also will become a concern.

Any time your use of debt rather than equity increases, or the size of your debt increases, it is time to pay attention. Let either go on too long, and your business may be in trouble.

This is another reason why a budget is crucial. You must be able to build a strong case that the injection of cash you get and the conditions required to repay it will enable you to move forward successfully. If that turns out not to be true, then going back to the well a second time is truly throwing good money after bad.

Performance Note
Stay out of the Triple-F Lending Institution!

This is especially true if the well is the Triple-F Well of Money: Friends, Family, and Fools are a questionable source of financing

141

to start with, but going back a second time is going to cost you relationships and credibility.

♫

So, When Is Debt A Good Thing?

When you use it as a tool for growth. Used right, debt can fuel a Great Performance in a business.

A business is like any other system: without the injection of energy (in the form of resources like money) it slows down and eventually runs out of steam. You can inject financial fuel in any number of ways, including:

- increasing sales;
- seeking investors or partners; and
- using debt.

What you don't have, when your goal is a Great Performance in your business, is the choice to do nothing.

Here are 4 reasons why debt can be the energy injection of choice to help you grow your business:

1. **Begin at the beginning.** In many business start-up situations you have significant expenses before you have the sales to pay for them. You have two choices: you can scramble, cut corners, and cut prices to generate volume, and reinvest your skinny profits back in your business while you wait 10 years to grow. Or you can get a loan, invest it where the money will make the most difference (specifically yield a greater rate of return than the interest on the debt), and focus on methodically growing your business. That could be the overture to a Great Performance!

2. **Cheap debt makes money.** When you weigh out things like the cost of equity, the cost of debt, and the adjustments to the true cost of debt after taxes, often you can expect a higher return than the cost of the debt incurred. This is true whether you are in start-up mode or not. Completely oversimplified, if you borrow at 10% and you can invest the funds into a business activity that yields 15%, you earn 5% on the money you borrowed. Like I said, oversimplified, but basically sound. One of the key factors in making that little story a reality is the impact of taxes (both deducted and owed). This is why before you take any steps to borrow significant amounts, or if you aren't sure whether you should be seeking equity from an investor or using debt, talk to your accountant!

3. **Everything in the sandbox remains yours...** Debt does not change your ownership or management position in the business. When you seek partners or investors there is almost always a loss of control or ownership on some level. When you use debt to grow your company, shy of your obligation to repay principal and interest, your company and your decisions remain 100% your own.

4. **...including the profits.** Not only does control of the company remain with you, the profits are yours too. Lenders don't require a share of your profits in exchange for a loan. As long as you make your payments, your profits stay in your jeans. When you work with investors, in many cases, the more you make, the richer they get.

Assuming you can build a valid case for using debt to grow your business, let's have a look at some of the positive ways to manage that debt.

♫

Making Small Business Debt Work

Debt is a tool. You can use it to make things happen by buying new equipment or buying out a competitor. You know the saying it takes money to make money? Well, this is one way to get that first money.

Consider equity. While using debt has its value, working with an investor may also have value. While using equity dilutes ownership (you usually exchange a percentage of ownership in the company for the money), it has the benefit of not eroding cash flow or restricting you from seeking other forms of financing. The loss of some degree of ownership (and sometimes management rights) must be weighed against the potentially high cost of servicing debt.

When you borrow money, you get to keep all the profits you *might* make as a result. When you work with an investor, you *may* get to keep all the money you would have had to use to service a debt. Careful planning and analyses will reveal which one is greater in your favour.

Plan. The planning for taking on debt is simple: what is the impact of debt servicing (principal and interest) on your cash flow? You also have to factor in possible revenue growth you have used the debt to leverage. If you are investing in something that will help you lower costs (such as a newer piece of equipment), factor in those savings as well.

To arrive at that net amount, always use the most conservative figure possible. This is not the time to look at the blue sky through rose-coloured glasses. By mixing two metaphors I hope I am communicating the importance of this! If you think that new display case will increase sales by 5% to 20%, use 5% as your number. Also, weigh the cost of debt against the lost opportunity cost of not making the acquisition, upgrade, or similar. This means if you don't invest in that display case, what will that cost your business? If the net positive difference between not acting and acting is greater than total cost of debt, go for it. If not, walk away.

Never go into debt for something that only may help. You can be very sure the bank will never tell you that you only might have to repay that loan.

Never lose sight of cash flow either. A big payoff from your debt-leveraged investment may happen in three years, but are you able to keep cash flow positive while you wait to get to that point?

Know your limit (and play within it). I use the slogan from various state and provincial lottery boards advisedly: few financing decisions are entirely risk free. Even the best plan can go sour when unpredictable weather has its way. Ensure that your budget has the headroom to let you make payments even if the debt-leveraged improvements completely fail to pay for themselves.

Again, it's personal. Many small-business owners have no business debt per se, but have personal debt. Personal debt still reduces flexibility to act in tough times. When the owner requires every possible penny of the business earnings to service a lifestyle and related debt (divorce can be a real killer in this way), there is little flexibility to leave money in the company to fuel growth. Get that personal debt under control.

Attack with snowballs. If you have a number of loans (business or personal), don't pay each debt off at the same rate. Attack your smallest debt or the one with the highest rate of interest first. By doing that you will have the greatest positive impact on your cash flow in the shortest amount of time. When you have paid off one debt, don't pocket the money you were using to pay it down. Take that monthly amount, and add it to the amount you are paying on the next smallest or highest interest debt until that in turn is paid off. Rinse and repeat. That technique of throwing a constant amount of money at debts even as they shrink, is called the *snowball* approach to debt repayment, and it works.

Consider all your masters. If the erosion of cash flow is the central challenge in managing debt, then constantly reviewing your payable accounts makes sense. Interest rates and terms are constantly changing across different debt instruments. If you can negotiate better pricing or better terms from suppliers you will improve your ability to service your debts. Remember when improving cash flow, time matters almost as much as dollar amounts. If you can get 60-day terms rather than 30 while keeping the same interest rates, for example, then you are ahead.

Don't rob Madison Avenue to pay Bay Street. A deliberately mixed geographic reference there. Madison Avenue in New York was the heartland of advertising in much of the 20th century. Bay Street in Toronto is the fabled home of the Canadian banking system.

If you have to cut back on your marketing (Madison Avenue) because you have to pay your loan debts (Bay Street), you may be in serious trouble. Reducing marketing may reduce growth, which in turn may reduce your ability to pay your debts. When businesses start slashing marketing programs, I know it won't be long before the vultures start circling.

Don't stick your head in the sand. Review your financial statements each month and micromanage the dollars, percentages, and ratios. When your debt costs begin to grow as a percentage of your revenues, even by a fraction of a point, it may be an early warning sign that your debts are switching from a lever for growth to an anchor around your neck. I'll say it again: budget carefully and watch your debt-to-equity ratio closely. Your banker will be.

Performance Note
Any credible creditor would rather have you
as a living customer than a bad statistic.

Keep your friends close (and your enemies closer). Great communication, and evidence that you are honouring your commitments goes a long way to helping you negotiate good debt servicing. Check in regularly with your creditors while things are still good and especially when you realize there may be challenges. Relationships matter, even in this situation. Keep in mind that a creditor would rather keep you as a living customer than as a bad statistic. When things do get tight, a creditor would rather get back something than nothing. Throwing you under the bus (calling your loan and potentially triggering bankruptcy) is a measure of last resort for a creditor, but you can hasten that moment through poor communication.

Debt is fire: extremely useful for making a tasty meal, but burns like hell if misused.

♫

Is It Worth It?

Sometimes in the search for that Great Performance, the resources available to us from within the company (called *bootstrapping*) just aren't enough. A great deal on a piece of equipment, or the chance to buy out a competitor, come along only so often. Most of the time, not only do we not have the cash on hand when that happens, it is not always even the best use of that cash if we had it. Sometimes using other people's money - at a reasonable rate of interest - is a more profitable strategy.

Remember the resource triangle: people, time, and money. One of the most powerful things debt can do is to shorten the time leg of the triangle by increasing the money leg. Sure we could achieve that Great Performance in 10 years, but if - with carefully managed debt - you could get there in 7, would it be worth it?

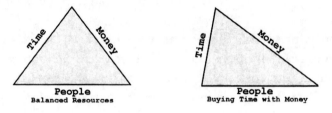

Of course it would. Just plan, and proceed carefully.

Journal Intermission

- Dream with debt. Note three areas in your business where a loan would make a big difference.

- Have you ever stared your debts in the face? If not, this is a great time to do it. Look at all of your combined business and personal debt and add up the interest charges each month. Now write down what you could do with that money to grow your business or bring pleasure to your personal life.

♫♫♫

Summary

Since the early days of civilization, people in business have turned to the gods and supernatural forces to aid them in their enterprises.

When you look at the forces that impacted small businesses, it is no surprise: changes in government, changes in weather, wars, pestilence, ruthless competition, new laws, fluctuations in currency, disruptions in trade routes, new inventions that rendered your business irrelevant overnight... The list of forces beyond the control of small-business owners goes on and on.

That hasn't changed. Many of the items that kept awake the small-business owners of ancient Greece or Egypt still plague us today, and the reliance on superstitions has not changed either. Where once it was fortune tellers, diviners, sacred blessings, and sacrifices, in the new world it is The Secret, Feng Shui, and economists. It is also the uncritical use of phrases like *time management*, *things happen* for a reason or *work-life balance*, and the belief in overnight success and secret formulas for creativity and productivity.

None of that is to say that ancient traditions like Feng Shui, or really seeking to understand what our work is and how it interacts with other aspects of our lives, may not yield some creative ways of living and doing business more successfully. When the book-sales-driving mix of pseudo-science, eastern religions, and sloppy use of language and logic become a substitute for understanding and employing the fundamentals of good business practices, we have a very serious problem—and we have the makings of a spectacularly bad Band Camp performance.

♫

The Art of Business

A dancer has his feet, a musician her voice or instrument, the filmmaker his story and camera, the playwright her actors and lights. When a guitarist hits a wrong note, or a dancer fumbles his steps, you don't hear them say, "It was meant to be."

When the silversmith or the novelist is up until 4 A.M. working on a creation of great beauty you don't hear them talk about wanting to improve their life-work balance over coffee the next morning. No. In the arts there is only the passionate love for the form, and the desire to perfect it every day. There is only practice. There are hours and blood and sweat and tears, and the company of all of those who share the journey.

A business seeking a Great Performance is no different. There is the love for what you do, which you could never imagine not doing. There is the desire to do better every day. There is the appreciation for the people: the customers and team members who share the journey with you.

Understand your discipline, and the basic building blocks of business. Study them every day. Seek to do a better job of using each one and integrating them ever more effectively. Put in your 10,000 hours.

There is no secret. There is nothing hidden from anyone who has the courage to look the world of business square in the face. There is magic, but it is no secret. It is the magic of people and communities using their creativity and the power of relationships to launch ideas into our world, and businesses into the stratosphere of success.

Your Great Performance only has 3 elements you can work with: People, Time, and Money. Nothing more; nothing less. Learn to master them by treating each with respect and honesty, and you will have fans cheering in the streets.

♪♪♪

Master Class: People, Time, And Money

Check the boxes as you go through this. These points are not optional. There is no Great Performance until you have checked off 100% of the boxes!

The *Do This Now* items are marked to indicate that if you do not have these in place in your business, forget the list, and do these now!

The day-to-day execution of these items would take another book to describe. That might be coming. In the meantime, hire a good business coach to guide you through these steps.

People

☐

1. Conduct a bottleneck assessment.

   a. Work with your team to **identify where the drags on efficiency are.** What is slowing things down.

   _____
   _____
   _____

   b. Do informal cost/benefit analyses to determine which improvements in operations would yield the biggest returns. Budget and schedule the changes. Decide where a dollar spent will yield the most returns and start there.

   _____
   _____
   _____

Time

☐

2. Create schedules and routines based on the 3-Cycle structure. Record them in your Standard Operating Procedure manual.

_____

_____

_____

a. Current Cycle. **Schedule 10 to 15 minutes each day to review operations.** Focus on efficiency, employee experience, and direct customer experience.

- Check in particular: Customer comments and feedback.
- Safety and ergonomics feedback from employees
- Are things displayed and communicated optimally? Were there any complaints about poor communication or negative surprises?
- Is there anything you can do to be even more respectful of your customers' time?
- If something went wrong, how was it handled?
- Consistency: note any deviations from standard procedure. This is not about enforcement, it is about what works. Be aware deviations may be a sign that the procedure or policy is not the best it can be. Review and act.

_____

_____

_____

b. Growth Cycle. **Schedule 1 hour each month and ½ day each quarter to review marketing.** These reviews must be team based (for example, meetings!) Check in on:

- Changes in the business environment.
- Your performance on the full Customer Experience Cycle.
- Trends emerging from your research and tracking.
- Larger financial trends.
- New directions, internally or externally, to reduce costs or improve the performance of your business in the market.
- From a customer perspective, are you providing a remarkable experience from the first point of contact, through the sale, and in your follow-up process?

_____

_____

_____

c. Deep Cycle. **Schedule 1-hour meetings every quarter and an annual retreat to review your internal and external situation,** and respond with long-term plans.

- Consider: are you discussing long-term evolutionary plans, or strategic revolutionary change?
- Keep the focus on who you want to be (individually or corporately) more than what you are going to be as a business.
- Spend some time discussing larger trends: politics, culture, business, and science. Review your organization and your plans in light of these trends.

- Develop some early operational action items that will steer your brand in the direction you wish to move. Review the role products, services, training, visual branding, operations, and other aspects might have on getting you to an accurately targeted rendezvous with your future.

Money

☐

3. **Get a Bookkeeper *Do This Now*** If you have never had a bookkeeper go through your finances, stop everything and find a good one now. Take your time, get referrals, but get it done.

☐

4. **When you have found your bookkeeper, set up a meeting schedule with her or him.** Ideally you should meet with your bookkeeper at least once a month. If you are a larger business, this relationship might be with your accountant or comptroller.

☐

5. If you have an accountant, meet with them quarterly, not just once a year at year end. If your accountant puts up roadblocks to make time to reflect on the finances of your business, get a new one. A good accountant should be a partner in the Great Performance of your business.

---

* Do This Now * Set up a business bank account. Even if your business is a sole proprietorship, you should never run your business finances through your personal bank account. Shop around. Some institutions still haven't figured out that we are in the 21st century and treat their business customers like parasites treat their hosts: sucking them dry. Not every institution is like this. Ask for referrals from friendly businesses. Decide carefully, but get this done.

☐

6. *** Do This Now * Pay yourself.** This means two things:

a. When you pay yourself, use a cheque from the company to yourself. This will make bookkeeping and financial planning infinitely simpler and more accurate. Do not use your business credit card, cheques, or debit card to pay for personal items.

---

b. Immediately set aside some of the money you pay yourself from the company, even if it is as little as $10 a week. Put it into a totally seperate account from your business and your other personal finances. The personal financial cushion that this builds up will give you a lot of security in coming years.

_____

_____

_____

☐
7. **Learn to read your Income Statement** (also called a Profit & Loss Statement), your Statement of Cash Flows, and your Balance Sheet. One sign you have engaged a good bookkeeper is they will be able to explain these records to you in a way that makes sense.

_____

_____

_____

☐
8. *** Do This Now * Create a budget.** Work with your bookkeeper, accountant, or a business coach to develop a planning budget for your business. Some considerations:

a. This is not a formal accounting document and is developed on a cash basis, not accrual basis.

_____

_____

_____

b. This planning document has many names, many of them starting with pro forma, meaning it is executed using a set of formal assumptions rather than reality. For my clients, I call them Coaching Financials or Planning Budgets.

_____

_____

_____

c. The budget tracks performance for one year, on a monthly basis.

_____

_____

_____

d. Planning budgets should have three parts to complete:

- Revenues and direct costs for each major business activity, division, SKU, and others, and a gross profit amount each month.
- Fixed or administrative costs, and a net profit for each month.
- All other cash outflows not otherwise captured, or 'hidden' on the balance sheet, like monthly debt servicing, owner's draws, etc.

_____

_____

_____

e. Carry forward the amount at the very bottom, after all three sets of expenses have had their way with your revenues, to the top of the next month as your starting cash. If it is a negative amount, you have some hard questions to ask, as there can be no negative amounts. A negative amount here means either you cannot pay your bills, or you have to dip into some form of debt to carry you through the month. How you calculate that into your budget is a question to ask your bookkeeper, accountant, or business coach.

_____

_____

_____

☐

9. **Set aside a fund for income tax and other government remittances.** Work with your accountant or bookkeeper to estimate what your remittances will be at the end of the year based on your budget, as a percentage of your revenues. Every week or every month, set aside that percentage of your revenues in a separate bank account. Then, when tax time comes, you won't have to scramble to pay your bill!

_____

_____

_____

☐

10. **Create shareable financial reports** you can use in planning meetings. These are best done as spreadsheets. Confidential items like employee compensation must be taken out of the picture, but it is critical for a Great Performance on the part of your team, and your whole business, that the key numbers are available.

_____

_____

_____

☐

11. Develop a long-term growth budget. This document should be part of your Deep Cycle planning process. What will the finances of your business look like 18 months to 10 years from now?

_____

_____

_____

☐

12. Review your cash flow weekly, or even daily. In particular, keep an eye on revenues and accounts receivable.

_____

_____

_____

☐

13. Examine your business for any opportunities to create subscriptions plans.
These can have a powerful positive influence on your monthly cash flow.

_____

_____

_____

☐

14. **Attack your personal debt.** ***Do This Now*** As a small business owner your personal finances have an impact on how your run your business.

_____

_____

_____

☐

15. **Schedule regular check-ins with your suppliers.** Don't assume the prices and terms you are paying are written in stone. It never hurts to ask if better terms can be arranged.

_____

_____

_____

An Addendum To Act II

The 3 Cycles: Their Musical Roots

I didn't want to weigh down the earlier discussion of the three Cycles with a technical dissection of how they relate to their musical inspiration. If you are still interested... read on here.

In acoustics we look at things like *frequency*, or cycles per second, and *period*, the distance between one peak in the wave and the next. The two are related.

A high musical note has a high frequency (measured in thousands or even tens of thousands cycles per second), and a short period.

A mid-frequency wave (think alto saxophone or the middle keys of a piano) has slower oscillations (the middle A key on a piano is 440 cycles per second) and longer periods.

In music the notes described as low, or bass notes, are measured in 10s of cycles. The lowest sound normally audible to humans is about 20 cycles per second, and the periods are far apart.

I have applied these cycles to business planning. The *frequency* is the pitch or busyness of the activity, and the *period* as a measure of how far into the future the planning cycle looks.

The Current Cycle has a high frequency—meetings and reviews happen daily—and a short period. It concerns itself with matters that happen every day. We turn on the lights, we care for our customers, we ship our products.

The Growth Cycle has a lower frequency—meetings and reviews happen monthly - and a longer period. The changes anticipated and planned for here happen over the weeks and months. New ads come out, new products are developed.

The Deep Cycle has the lowest frequency—meetings and review happen quarterly and annually—and the focus is on a very long period between peaks: every 18 months to 10 years. Organizations switch from selling soft drinks to franchising restaurants, or from selling computer to providing information services.

Just like in music the behavior of each cycle impacts the other cycles in ways that are either harmonious: they reinforce each other's contribution to that Great Performance or they are dissonant. They make competing demands on resources and they support conflicting agendas. That gives you all the elements of a Band Camp performance.

To achieve that great performance always write the bass line first. Get a sense of the Deep Cycle directions of your business, and then write the Growth and Current Cycle parts. Where Stephen Covey meets Miles Davis: *begin with the bass line in mind!*

♫♫♫

ACT III:
PLANNING YOUR EXIT

Performance Note
"Begin with the end in mind."
Stephen Covey

What's It All Worth?

However you measure the year-by-year return of your business, whether you measure salary, owner's draw, profits, retained earnings, do you ever feel like none of it quite adds up to what you put into it?

Do friends and family ask: *"Why do you have your own business? We just don't see what you get for the 14 hours a day, 5, 6, or 7 days a week, and all that stress you put into it."* That question is one that most owners have no idea how to answer. They mumble things about *"being my own boss"* or *"working my own hours"* or *"creating my own opportunities"*. Anyone who owns a small business knows the first two just aren't true. When you own your own business, your customers are your boss, and the demands of your business set your hours, not you.

The last answer about creating your own opportunities is closer to the truth, but too often even that just isn't the way you thought it would be.

The Real Answer

Here is the real answer. *"I have my own business because it lets me work in something I love, to create something I have dreamed of, and provide for my family. When I have finished with it, I will find an exit that helps me fund whatever I decide to do next."*

That last part, the part about the exit, is almost never part of the answer for most business owners. It must be if you want that *ultimate* Great Performance for your business. You must build your business to the point where you can leave it partially or completely and realize the rest of the enormous investment you have made in your business over the years. Act III will show you why and how this last act is central to any Great Performance.

Act III is about departures, exits, wind-downs, and phasings-out of all sorts. For a truly Great Performance, almost from the moment your business is established, you should be finding ways to remove yourself from it. You begin by finding ways to delegate and take your hands off the tools one day at a time.

The first scene in Act III will look at the whys and hows of taking your hands off the tools and switching from orchestra member to conductor; from camera operator to director.

This is critically important for two simple reasons:

1. You cannot grow the business to Great Performance stature when you are spending every day being chief, cook, and bottle washer; and
2. You cannot realize the full value of your business as long as its growth and value are limited by the hours you can spend in it.

Great Performances require the highest level of leadership. The time required, the habits of mind, and the focus needed for that level of leadership are incompatible with spending every day in the shop.

Act III

The last scene in Act III will help you realize the ultimate value of your business: its sale. Why is the sale so important? Let me put this as plainly as I can: the dollars earned by you and your business in the 10, 15, or 20 years you own it only represent part of its potential return. The total return on the time and money, blood, sweat, and tears you put into it are difficult to realize in the time you own the business.

The ultimate return on all of your sacrifices may not be realized until you sell (or franchise, license, develop partnerships, etc.). As is so often the case, the kinds of things you do to prepare for long-term success also yield great returns in the short term.

The process of organizing your business, documenting what matters, learning how to delegate and develop partnerships for the long term, will all improve the satisfaction and return you realize now. Let's get started.

♫♫♫

The Case Stories

Band Camp Performance

Ray was 67 and tired. He had been in the electrical business for almost 40 years, and had owned his own company, Stellar Electric, for the last 23. He had 7 employees, and the business supported his family well. It wasn't a bad run, but it was time to get out. Ray had never been that great with the books, and he didn't have much patience with marketing. He believed firmly if you did good work, people would recommend you to their neighbours. The Yellow Pages took care of the rest. While that had worked well for the first 15 or so years, the last few had been harder. Times were tough.

Employees weren't what they used to be. In the last few years Ray had difficulties keeping good electricians, and a couple of incompetent ones had cost him some money. Labour costs were getting harder to keep up with. About two years ago, a supplier had closed Stellar Electric's account because Ray was increasingly behind on paying his bills; two others had done the same last year. As long as he ignored that situation, his cash flow wasn't bad. He always made payroll and paid himself enough to keep the wolf from the door.

But it was exhausting, so when an offer came in from a younger competitor to buy the company, Ray jumped at the chance. He hoped to make a bit of money to retire on, but mostly he just wanted out.

Initially Ray asked $240,000 for the business, but by the time the lawyers and accountants were done, all that the buyer was prepared to offer was $140,000, part of which was contingent on him sticking around to manage things in transition for 6 months. It wasn't what he wanted, but Ray was too tired to fight it; besides, the bills were piling up again. He took the offer.

On May 1 of that year, after 6 months of helping with the transition, Ray took his cheque for just under $100,000 for the assets of Stellar Electric, shook hands with the new owner, and headed home. $100,000 for 23 years of his life. Not what he had hoped.

♫

Great Performance

Bookkeeping, done right, is a crazy business. Steph knew that because she had been doing it for the past 27 years. Sometimes it had been a blast, sometimes it was exhausting, and sometimes she didn't know if she could do it anymore; for many days, it had been all three. Steph was turning 58 next year and already knew when she packed up her office to go on her regular post-tax-season holiday it would be for the last time. She was selling the business, something she had been preparing for, for the last 17 years.

At about the 10-year mark of owning Balanced Bookkeeping Services, Steph knew she could not continue as she was indefinitely. The hours were too long, and if she ever got sick or wanted to take some time off, the business would grind to a halt. She could see then, if she didn't change something, she was going to be doing data entry when she was 75. Steph had seen too many of her clients in this situation and it wasn't fun to watch.

Consulting with the various business support people in her environment at the time, Steph developed an exit plan: in 15 years she was going to have something she could sell, or at least pass on to be managed by someone else while she retained ownership. Steph incorporated the business, and got to work.

Over the years Steph built her business to a team of 8. About 10 years ago, she had bought the building she was in and rented out the space she didn't need to a mortgage broker, a small accounting firm, and a local environmental consultancy.

In that pivotal year when she decided to develop the exit plan, Steph had also learned she needed to shift her focus from working *in* the business as a bookkeeper to actively owning, managing, and growing the business. She hired staff that shared her values and she invested heavily in training. One key employee was an administrator she hired about four years into *the program* (as she called it). Diane wasn't the first administrator she hired, but she was the one that finally proved to be what she needed.

Together Steph and Diane developed policies and procedures that covered most of what went on in the business. It took a few years, but by the time they were done, the business almost ran itself on a day-to-day basis. Everyone was able to take holidays, and staff turnover was low. Customers received the same level of service regardless who was handling their account.

From the added revenues, subtract the cost of the administrator. The calculations are simplistic, but you would be ahead $8,000.

3. **Outsource.** Even if you have accepted the cost of labour is a good investment, having employees can be a huge challenge. Designing the job and roles, recruiting, training, retaining, managing, are all difficult and time-consuming for most small-business owners. Fortunately, hiring is not the only way. Consider engaging professionals on contract for fixed monthly rates or piecework. A very common (and hugely helpful) place to start is with your bookkeeping. I know very few business owners who are passionate about doing their own books. Move it on. Bookkeeping, cleaning, IT services, filing, delivery, are all activities that you can contract someone to do at a reasonable rate.

4. **Review your pricing.** Yes, pricing has a significant impact on this challenging area.

Performance Note
Discount pricing can lock you
into a permanent hamster-wheel
of working in the business.

Pricing from a place of understanding your value to your customers begins an important positive-feedback loop. When you commit to exceptional products and customer service, and charge accordingly, it enables you to hire staff. With the improved focus and increased time available, you are able to provide even greater value for your customers, justifying the prices you are charging. This is a classic positive-feedback loop. If I had to pick one marketing function that most locks

Diane was now a partner in the business.

Balanced Bookkeeping Services was consistently profitable, had virtually no debt on the books, and had seen revenue growth between 12% and 18% every year for the last decade. If she wasn't selling, she would seriously have considered opening up another office in a neighbouring community to deal with the unending demand.

All that growth, structure, and stability was worth a great deal to the buyers, Diane and her husband. By the time everything settled out Steph would see about $800,000 from the sale.

Life wasn't going to stop there; Steph had other irons in the fire. For now, she was looking forward to packing up her office and taking that very much extended holiday she was planning.

♫♫♫

Taking The Long View

In Act II of this book we explored the three cycles of business. I stressed that a Great Performance is only achieved when all three cycles are included in the planning processes, and have an equal place on the calendar of the organization.

One way of looking at your journey towards a Great Performance as a business owner is you must always be seeking ways to move your focus from the first (Current) cycle to the third (Deep) cycle. You can only do this by delegating the Current Cycle work to others, because it still needs to be done, and done brilliantly.

With each passing month you must be finding ways to move your focus from daily operational details to the long-term growth and health of your business.

Performance Note
*A Great Performance requires you
to stop 'doing' and start leading.*

Here is the rule for a Great Performance in this area: *the greater your leadership responsibilities, the less you should be spending on the Current Cycle.*

Current Cycle work is what you have employees and team members for; if you don't have them, it is a primary responsibility to get them in place over time. If you are the owner and you are spending more than 30%, or an hour or two of your days, on the shop floor, we need to grow your team.

If you are an independent professional who measures billable hours (consultant, stylist, coach, physiotherapist, lawyer) does this still apply to you? Yes, it does. Clearly your billable hours are the foundations of your business, particularly at the beginning, but there will come a time when you hit a ceiling. When you are working as many hours as you can, your waiting list is full, and you are charging the maximum you can in your market.

You may think you have *made* it at that point, but don't let your guard down. Even in that scenario, you will still not be extracting the maximum return on your business, you will still not be able to sell it for its true value, and if you get sick or even want to take an extended holiday, that is not going to be possible.

You still need to find a way to move out of the focus on the current cycle of your business *or you will be at that level for the rest of your career.* All of this is rooted in one basic understanding: all the money *you* can make on an hourly basis alone will almost never represent all the value captured, or bottled up, in your business.

That money, or that value, represents the true return on the years of working, stressing, and sacrificing that you have done. So we need to get that value out!

This has two implications:

1. **You must find some way of earning a passive income.**
    Passive income, or what one of my teachers once referred to as money while you sleep, unhooks you from the slavery of

the clock. This is revenue that flows into your business even when you are not at work.

2. **You must find some way of building your business as an asset with growing value for the future.** Failing to do that is like keeping your money under the mattress instead of investing it in something the yields a return: all you get is what you make. I have yet to meet a business owner who thinks what they are taking out of the business right now fairly compensates them for what they are putting in.

♫

You can't do any of this alone.

As we did in Act I of *Great Performances*, we begin again with the power of people.

You need people to:

1. Take on the Current Cycle activities of your business so that you can focus on long-term growth and your ultimate exit;
2. Help you create passive income streams, either as employees who keep the business running when you aren't there, or as strategic partners, like consultants and publishers, who can help you develop alternate revenue streams like books and websites; and
3. Help you build your business as investors, managers, and other employees.

♫♫♫

SCENE 11: The Owner Lets Go To Grow!

Performance Note
*"The great leaders are like the best conductors -
they reach beyond the notes to reach the magic in the players."*
Blaine Lee

Band Camp Performances:

Limiting your business to the time, vision, skills, and other
energies that you alone bring to the table.

Great Performances:

Creating layers of networks, teams, and partnerships that act
as levers to help you grow your business far beyond anything
you could do alone.

♫

Ride A New Cycle

As we learned in Act II, the Current Cycle is about delivering
on the sales you have already made. It is all about executing and
operations.

I have watched many small-business owners get lost in
this world. I see them clinging to the levers and the tools,
micromanaging the day-to-day operations of the business to
the detriment of its growth and their own physical and mental
health. Deeply successful business owners understand that their
best place is managing the Growth and Deep Cycles.

It is a daily reality for many small-business owners that, at least
in the beginning, they do have to do everything. As time passes,
and demand grows, if the owner does not begin to focus their
time on designing and structuring the future of her business, the

business will never grow. There are a limited number of hours and only two hands. In a classic case of diminishing returns, the fatigue and stress will increase as you work harder and harder to stay on top of everything.

The dangers of this are the stress, the financial restrictions, and the sure knowledge the business will never develop to the point where it lets the owner move on to other things or to retire.

As long as the formula is you = *the business*, you can never leave.

The first step out of this is to delegate.

I Can't Afford That!

I have worked with many business owners who claimed they couldn't afford the help. Nonsense. Upon examination, not once has that claim held up as stated. The truth is that the owners are afraid to let go.

A business that truly has no ability to invest in the human levers it requires to grow will never yield the full return on the owner's investment. If there really is no hope of ever having the business activities and sales volume to support more than one person, it is worth asking if the business will ever really be what you dreamed it would. That sounds harsh, but consider the alternative: are you prepared to be Ray from the *Band Camp Performance* at the head of Act III?

Starting Your Casting Call

How do you begin growing that cast of great performers? What can a small business do to begin the process of delegating work to let the owner focus on growing the business?

How can an owner begin that shift in focus from the Current Cycle to the Deep Cycle?

Performance Note

"The one thing you need to know about personal success:
discover what you don't like doing, and stop doing it."
Marcus Buckingham

Here are 7 suggestions:

1. **Know your strengths.** This is where it starts. As the owner, where do you add the most value to your organization? Are you the source of creative ideas? Do you make beautiful things or do great original work with your hands? Are you a sales rainmaker? Are you a great communicator and motivator? Discover the one thing you do better than anything else, focus on doing just that, and commit to finding people to do the rest.

2. **Know what you are worth.** Your strengths must have value measurable in dollars. Whatever it is you do brings value to the business. If you are the lead sales person, or a crafts or trades person, your value is clear: it is the revenue you bring into the business as a direct result of your activities. Even if you are the manager or leader or chief networker, you have to find a way to determine what that activity is worth for the business. If you stopped doing it, what would happen to the business? If you had to hire someone to replace you exactly, what would you have to pay in your market? If you can account for what you are worth to the business, you can take the next step and download lower value activities to others at the right price. For example, if you know that as a networker or rainmaker you can bring in $10,000 per month in revenues but you spend half of your time on the administration of your business, then hiring a part-time administrator at $2,000 per month just makes financial sense. If you could double your time, you could bring another $10,000 into the business.

owners into having a job rather than running a business, it is underpricing.

5. **Consider part-time.** How much time would you gain if you hired a high-school student for a couple of hours to help you out with administrative, operational, or production tasks? I'm guessing probably enough time to give you a good return on your investment. In many jurisdictions, part-time labour arrangements also provide some breaks for the employer in the areas of benefits, employer contributions, etc. It is unethical to exploit these considerations (by doing things like laying off people just before they qualify for benefits, or keeping your weekly staffing hours just below the level where certain considerations are owed), but used properly part-time labour can free up you and other key employees to engage in higher-value work, and create further employment opportunities in your business. Another positive-feedback loop!

6. **Explore internships, co-ops, and wage subsidies.** Again, the word is explore, not exploit. If you have a good fit and the time to train, there are a number of avenues to access federal, provincial, or state programs for retraining workers on government subsidies. Universities and technical programs often have internship and coop programs for their students. These can be a cost-effective way for you to build your team, and to screen for potential long-term employees.

7. Finally, **reconsider your business model.** Perhaps the structure you have (mom & pop; bricks & mortar; sole proprietorship) simply doesn't allow you the flexibility or resources to grow. Time to rethink your business.

From the shop floor, employees sometimes wonder what managers and leaders do in that slow motion world they seem to inhabit. The answer is that good leaders make the future. You cannot do that in a hurry.

You cannot make great decisions about what is truly important and what is a passing crisis when you are moving too fast. If you are truly spending the majority of your days on the Growth and Deep Cycles of your business, your rhythms should reflect that. Slow down to plan, execute with care, and reflect.

Every Great Performance requires a great script or score. When you hear a violinist playing an incredibly rapid, high-energy passage in a musical score, it is easy to forget that passage took hours—even days—to write, and just as long to practice.

In business it is the same. Often what is executed quickly (like the preparation of brilliant meals in a busy restaurant) is planned very slowly. When you create breathing room around your commitments so you can think, plan, and create, it is called padding. The best example of padding is meetings. Don't book your meetings into the very tightest time possible. Allow time for getting there and setting up, for the meeting to take the time appropriate for the content, and to debrief and take notes when it's over. If you are rushing from one meeting to the next, not only are you likely to be late, you are not likely to be present, focused, or creative. Pad your schedule generously.

When you align and group your activities and priorities into like categories and large blocks of time, it is called chunking. Chunking has two benefits: it forces you to pick what matters and assign single blocks of time to it; and it builds the Great Performance discipline of creating true focus in your activities. A simple example is email. Instead of letting email distract you by doing it whenever (which usually means when

Performance Note

Setting up the right business model
frees you to make more money
and sets you up for a Great Exit.

Have you considered second locations? Franchising? An online store? Incorporation and additional shareholders and investors? Have you considered buying out a competitor? Not only might these options create some elbow room for growth, they will also start you down the road of the succession and exit planning.

Many of these options seem daunting and like they are "just not for me". Don't let them scare you. There are many resources out there to support small businesses that can help you with the challenging process of expanding your business.

Even with the help, the process is never simple or easy. But if you don't begin it you will never help your business achieve that Great Performance.

♫

Journal Intermission

- What are you best at? What do you least like doing?

- If you could bring one person into your business to let you focus on growing your business, what would that person do?

- What job could a part-time high school student do for you to make a difference?

♫♫♫

SCENE 12: The Owner Manages What Matters

Performance Note
*"Decide what you want,
decide what you are willing to exchange for it.
Establish your priorities and go to work."*
H. L. Hunt

Band Camp Performances:

Spending every day taking care of business; being focused on the Current Cycle; moving from crisis to crisis, always responding, seldom initiating.

Great Performances:

Setting priorities that will grow the business, and sticking to them; leading your team by exercising your strengths; developing a team that takes care of all the rest; initiating more than reacting.

♫

What Matters Most?

Once you have those employees or team members in place, then what? How do you know where to put your energies? What truly matters?

Performance Note
As a leader what matters most to you is the future.

Your job as the leader is to make the biggest and deepest decisions about the future of your business. To do this you must have support from others in taking care of the present of your business.

Given that, the first answer should be clear: what you should do to manage your priorities is focus on the Growth and Deep Cycles of your business. The focus of these cycles was explored in Act II.

Marketing, networking, creating alliances, shaping the future of your brand, and always keeping in mind the ultimate end of all this: your exit strategy. For our purposes here, those are your primary focuses in the Growth and Deep Cycles.

Let's Start

1. **Commit to a vision.** Until you know where you are going, you won't know what your priorities are. If you are only responding to the crises and urgencies of each day, you aren't managing, you are being managed. Every true priority in your business must be ultimately linked to the end strategy. To start forging that chain backwards from that future to the present, you must know exactly what and where that future is.

2. **Cover the 3 cycles.** If you manage only for immediate priorities, you are a twig in the river; manage only for the long-term future and you'll be blind to the present. You must consider both the present and the future, and deliberately assign time for each of the three cycles: taking care of operations, marketing, and the long-term growth of your business and brand.

Performance Note
Everything needs to get done,
but you don't need to do everything.

3. **Create lists.** On paper or on your computer, capture everything that needs doing.

Stop making excuses like, "I don't need to write stuff down, it's just crazy busy right now, and things will get back to normal." No, they won't. Now is normal. Deal with it.

You can't remember everything, so start making lists. While you are at it, have a look at those lists and check to see that you are spending some time each week or month on each of the three cycles.

Note I suggested you create lists not take care of the lists.

When you create lists on those three levels, it puts you in charge. Those lists are developed into your Standard Operating Procedures and formal Growth Plans. You are working to become the creator of your future, rather than the puppet of your crazy present.

Performance Note
Use lists to write your future.

In the act of writing things down, you make them more real. You make yourself more accountable. You must confront each action item and decide whether it is for you to do or someone else. Lists write the future. Seen that way, there is nothing trivial or tedious about them. Each item on a list is (or should be) one small step to getting you to the vision you have created.

4. **Use chunking and padding.** Don't wedge activities tightly into every available minute of time. Life will do that to you anyway. Anticipate that and structure your time into large, generous blocks of related activities (like client time or writing time). This commits time to the priorities you have identified, and leaves breathing room so when the inevitable crises hit, you aren't as rattled by them because you aren't dealing with a teetering pile of commitments you can't honour.

you are avoiding something important), set aside clear chunks of time for it. I generally do my emails for about 20 minutes first thing in the morning (I know, many productivity experts say this is not a time I should give up to email, but it works for me and my clients), and for about 1 hour later in the afternoon. I have chunked client contact time, writing time, office administration time, networking time, etc. Most of these chunks are half days, which means my chunks are padded!

5. **Learn your rhythms.** Not everyone has a 4-hour attention span. I don't. While switch-tasking is unproductive for some, it works for others. I know I work best in 20 to 90 minute sprints. Then I have to go do something different, preferably something out of my chair. Going for a quick walk is awesome.

   Pay attention to how you work, and learn to build a structure around that. When you are clear on where you are going, when you use lists, schedules, and budgets to get you there, and you know how you work best, then you know how to execute your priorities in the most effective way. Are some things more routine? Schedule them when you know you have less energy. Do some priorities require your full creative focus? Schedule them when you know you are at your freshest.

6. **Plan with your team.** Don't set your priorities by yourself. Strategize with others. While you might have the clearest sense of where your company is going, you cannot know or act on all the thousands of details that will get you there. You will miss connections, miss opportunities, and not appreciate the true cause-and-effect relationship of every action you decide on.

Scene 12

Performance Note
Own your vision but execute with your team.

The best teams formulate priorities based on a mutual respect for unique perspectives and points of view. Your finance person will see the financial implications of planned actions better than you will. Your managers on the shop floor will see the impacts of your planned actions on front-line staff better than you will. Listen, adjust, and move towards your vision together.

Visions are generally single points, but the priorities that get you there must fit into a multitude of causes, possible consequences, and secondary effects impacted by the "weather" inside and outside the organization.

Managing all this is not something to do alone.

♫

Journal Intermission

- Write out a vision for the next big thing or step or change in your business. Be detailed: use numbers, colours, names, places. Make it as real as you can. Write in the present tense.

- List 2 – 3 specific activities that would grow the long-term future of your business, not just what needs to get done for tomorrow.

- Pay attention to how you work. What is your personal attention span?

♫♫♫

SCENE 13: Every Great Performance Is Worth Recording

Band Camp Performance:

Almost none of the good stuff you do is written down. When a key employee leaves, half of "the way we do things" leaves with her; when you hire a new employee he gets a different set of instructions than the last new hire did. A buyer for your business would have no idea how to assign value to what you do because no one can figure out what you do.

Great Performance:

Everything that matters is written down. When someone leaves, a new hire reviews the written roles and responsibilities and is up to speed on the basics in days. When you are ready to sell your business, your Standard Operating Procedures is so complete it is a valuable asset, and a significant part of the value of your business.

♫

The Design Of A Great Performance

Performance Note
Increasing routine increases the space to be creative.

Here is one of the paradoxes of Great Performances: they happen entirely in the moment, yet they are the result of years of design and preparation.

The moment that first note comes from the saxophone is like no other moment that will ever be. Influences, like the mood of the player, exactly how deep a breath he took, the mood of the audience, the acoustics of the room, are something the player and audience have little or no control over, and will never happen exactly that way again. Yet that ephemeral moment is the result of the deepest commitment, the most careful design, a profound passion for getting it right, and thousands of hours of hard and disciplined work.

In business, it is no different. Structured, well-designed systems and relentless, consistent hard work are the necessary foundations for the creativity, and flexibility, confidence and moment-by-moment brilliance that are the hallmarks of a Great Performance.

I know that sounds like Orwellian doublespeak, "Obedience is freedom." Yet, every musician, dancer, actor, and every participant in a religious community has known and understood that paradox for centuries. Knowing and practicing the rules truly is the foundation for anything great, whether in business, the arts, or the spiritual disciplines.

♫

It's A Monk's Life

The great monastic traditions of Europe and Asia have long understood that the rules are not there to bind the soul. They are there to free it.

The reason you get up to pray or meditate at the same time every day; why you eat at the same time and at the same place with the same rituals; why there are labyrinths and prayer beads; is because when the mundane is made routine it frees the heart and the soul to contemplate what truly matters.

It is hard to focus on the divine when you are wondering what to have for dinner tonight, or stressing about what to wear tomorrow. The same applies to Great Performances in business.

To focus on what will truly grow your business over the long term you must:

1. Identify what is trivial, mundane, or appropriate to the Current Cycle, and
2. Make it routine, make rules, design a system, and write it down.

Performance Note
*"I merely took the energy it takes to pout
...and wrote some blues"*
Duke Ellington

Happy To Have The Blues

The paradox of *freedom out of structure* is at the heart of the world's improvisational traditions in the performing arts. Whether it is the classical music of northern India, the American Blues, or improvisational theatre, there are rules. There is not one tradition of improvisation that teaches "do what you want."

In each tradition, the basics are the same: you must first learn the building blocks and the basic structures, and then you can truly play.

Great improvisation is the result of taking the basic building blocks of notes, rhythms, phrases, melody fragments, stories, and structures and recombining and juxtaposing them in unexpected ways. The 12-bar blues for example, are based on 3 harmonies repeated or 12 bars (or measures). That's it. Yet that profoundly simple structure is the basis of hundreds of thousands of performances for over 100 years—and not one performance was ever the same.

♫

When you, your employees, and your customers know what the rules are, what the values and boundaries are, it creates the freedom to allow each moment to unfold within that safe, consistent framework.

The reverse is very clear: failures in performance, in how a moment is handled, are almost always the consequence of poorly conceived and written policies, poor hiring, or poor training.

Accidents happen, but not as often as we would like to tell ourselves. Most failures are due to poor design and planning, or no planning at all. Also, any time someone says. *"I'm sorry. We can't do that. That's policy."* An alarm should go off. Sometimes that is an appropriate response, but when policy becomes an excuse or a consistent obstacle to great customer or employee experience, a deeper look is instantly required.

Policies do not restrict Great Performances; absent or bad policies restrict Great Performances.

♫

The Script For A Great Performance: The SOP

The joke is that men refuse to read them, but sometimes instructions and directions can come in really handy! All the more so when you are running a small business.

At the heart of the structure for a Great Performance, and the written documentation of that structure, is the Standard Operating Procedure (SOP) manual. It is also called an Operating Manual, or Policies and Procedures Manual. The name isn't that important. There is no reason why you can't call it *The Book of How We Do Stuff.*

SOPs are critical to a Great Performance in business because they are *the process and the record* of everything that matters that can be planned, designed, repeated, made routine, etc. A Standard Operating Procedure is valuable when an employee exits, because it makes transitions (like training replacements) more of classical music is the result of a brilliant interpretation of a brilliant score.

Performance Note

In a symphony orchestra, everyone is on the same page.

The score is the point of departure for all conversation and communication about the performance. When the clarinetist plays a C instead of a C#, she is not disregarding the conductor's instructions, she is disregarding the score.

The orchestral world is probably the source of the phrase *"everyone on the same page."* Literally.

In the business world, a SOP should play the same role: it is a document that lets communication take place on shared understandings, and common information. No surprises, and little room for the idiosyncrasies of our strange personalities.

The ability to reduce conflict is so much greater when you are able to say, *"The instructions for how that should have been done are on page 37"* rather than, *"I think this is how that should have been done because I am your boss."* That is not to say there won't be disagreements and unusual interpretations of written procedures. You have only to listen to 6 different pianists interpret a Beethoven sonata, where every note is written down, to hear just how differently we can be in our interpretation of a score. Those differences are a far cry from the chaos of personalities, approaches, habits, and prejudices that would otherwise be the foundation of how things get done (or don't get done!).

Whose mistake was that? A good SOP does not just prevent employees or new trainees from making stuff up as they go along. It should do the same for management. A good SOP is a tool for reducing arbitrary or vindictive management behaviors. It is important for an employee to be able to point out that what is being asked of them is outside effective and less costly. A Standard Operating Procedure is also a powerful tool when *you* pull back from the daily operation of the business, seek partners, or exit entirely.

SOPs are critical in the successful sale of a business. Here's how that should go when it happens perfectly: the previous owner closes up shop for the last time on a Friday night, hands the new owner the keys and the operating instructions (the SOP). The new owner opens up on Monday morning, turns on the lights, and gets to the business of making money. Ideally, it should be that simple.

When understanding the role of a Standard Operating Procedure in a business, this is the standard we are striving for: a document that tells every new employee *everything* they need about how the business runs, and exactly what is expected of them, and how their role fits into the other parts of the business. It tells a new owner *everything* they need to know to successfully run the business.

SOP Or Franchise Manual?

The ultimate form of a Standard Operating Procedure is a franchise manual. This is the documentation that describes every possible area of a business to a new franchise holder, as well as setting out the guidelines, expectations, and obligations that come with owning a franchise.

Where a typical SOP might be 10 to 40 pages in length, a franchise manual can be from 100 to 1000 pages. So where does the one end and the other begin? One way of looking at it is the Standard Operating Procedure would form the heart of a franchise manual.

The whole point of franchising is that you describe and package a successful business model to reproduce it in other locations and markets. The way to do this is to standardize the brand and operations of the business as much as possible. This ensures that each franchise location operates as much as possible like every other one. This forms the core value proposition of any franchise. It is why someone would buy a franchise rather than start a business from scratch: a successful franchise is a proven model that has been standardized to the point where you can reproduce the success just about anywhere, without having to reinvent the wheel.

So standardization is the heart of franchising and the SOP is the heart of standardization. It is both *the process and the documenting* of that standardization.

The goal for the SOP is to identify every single thing in a business that could be repeated, and standardize it. Whether it is cooking food, training employees, or answering the phone, if it happens more than once, it should happen as consistently as possible. Documenting that consistency to ensure it happens regardless of who is working or who is in charge is the main objective of a Standard Operating Procedure manual.

A franchise manual takes that SOP and wraps much more around it. Where the SOP only looks at those things that are generally repeated in a business, a franchise manual tries to look at everything, including those things that happen rarely, or even only once.

As well as daily operating procedures, a franchise manual can cover things like site selection, how to handle a grand opening, marketing guidelines, public relations, and health and safety guidelines. Just the table of contents alone for a franchise manual can be longer than the complete SOP for some businesses.

♫

Ready To Perform?

Performance Note
*If you had to see a lender, investor, or buyer
this Friday, would your business be ready?*

So why does all this matter to a small business owner?

Because one of the hallmarks of a Great Performance business is that it is "ready to be sold this Friday."

Selling, franchising, seeking investors, or obtaining a loan, the point is that Great Performance businesses are in a permanent state of readiness. Everything is ship shape, and everything that matters is documented. It is like the practice of surprise inspections in the military. If you never know when the inspection is coming, you create a permanent state of readiness and you are always operating at your best. That is a profound benefit whether you are exiting tomorrow, or performing for maximum profit and minimum stress for the next 25 years.

Remember the story of Ray at the beginning of this Act? His was a business run exclusively for his day-to-day needs, with very little regard for the future, and no preparation at all for an exit. When the day finally came for that exit, nothing was ready. Consequently, not only did Ray not receive what he should have for his business when it came time to exit, *it had not been profitable for years.*

Putting off to the future the work of being ready for anything is a Band Camp practice. If you are not ready to "sell on Friday," you are not getting the return on investment for your blood, sweat, and tears now either. On the other hand, when you operate with the end in mind, you reap benefits *right now* as well.

♫

Creating That SOP

So how do you begin the process of creating a Standard Operating Procedures manual? The initial steps are simple:

1. **Clarify practices and roles.** A Standard Operating Procedure is the written record of the successful practices unique to your business. Turning on the lights in the morning is nothing to write about. If you look around and discover there is nothing you do that is unique, we have another problem! Clarify what works, what is unique and must be captured, and who does what.

2. **Make the most of mistakes.** One of the secrets to creating a SOP is to note every time a mistake is made and what corrective action was taken. How will you ensure that mistake never happens again? Write its correction into your procedures. Doing this is not a guarantee of perfection, but it is pretty hard to justify a repeated mistake that is addressed in your manual!

3. **Capitalize on ignorance.** Want to know what to write down? How about everything you find yourself constantly repeating to your existing employees, and training into your new employees?

   It is as a training resource that a Standard Operating Procedure manual finds one of its greatest immediate values in a business. As we discovered in Act II, time is a business's most precious resource, and directing a new employee to read and internalize the important procedures in your business can be a huge time saver during the on-boarding and training process.

Here are some more tips for creating your SOP:

- **Review two key cycles.** I introduced the Current and

Growth Cycles in Act I. The first concerns itself largely with operations, and the second with marketing.

Review everything in your Current cycle: ordering, inventory procedures, different manufacturing processes, safety rules, preparation and clean-up, how things are measured and accounted for, etc. Confirm those unique best practices with your team and write them down.

Also, review with your team every routine you use to promote to customers, to close sales with customers, and to retain your customers. These are all Growth Cycle activities. Determine what constitutes best practices and write them down.

- **Take notes!** I am as big a fan of notebooks as I am the avowed enemy of the sticky note (that's another story). I believe every employee should have an inexpensive notebook in which to record the great ideas and cringe-worthy disasters of their work lives. When someone sees how something could be done better, write it down. More good ideas and solutions to problems are lost because the moment passes and with it the motivation for change.

  Dollar-store notebooks are a great investment, and should be mandatory to bring to every staff meeting!

- **Autobiographies.** Especially when it comes to job descriptions and front-line or shop-floor routines, have the people in the job write out what it is they do. When you review these notes and write them into your SOP, there is a great opportunity for a conversation. You may be surprised at how your employees see their jobs, and at their perceptions of what goes on. These are all teachable moments, both for you and for them. A great Standard Operating Procedure manual is never an ivory tower exercise. It should be rooted in real people's jobs, and policies and procedures that actually work.

- **A great SOP is a musical score.** A score is the written document of a piece of orchestral music. A great performance standard procedures. But if the management request is a good idea, then it should probably be captured in the Standard Operating Procedures.

Flash Point

The power of a Standard Operating Procedure manual in these situations brings up an important point: any policies and procedures that might come into play in the disciplining or termination of an employee should be vetted by a Human Resources specialist, or a lawyer specializing in business, contract, or labour law. You have to be extremely careful any time you say to an employee, especially in writing "Thou shalt...".

Furthermore, failure to follow a Standard Operating Procedure can be grounds for disciplinary action, and you need to be very sure that what you have written, and how it is enforced, is legal.

- **You need a goal.** While it may seem a surprise for such an operational document, it is important your SOP captures the big picture of your business as well.

For one thing, your SOP should contain your company mission statement. For another, your SOP needs to be designed with a clear purpose in mind. Structure and regimentation for their own sake are as negative as no structure at all. When you create a policy or written procedure, there has to be a reason for it.

Take the time to consider what it is you are trying to do with your SOP overall, and for each section. Are you driving for greater profitability? Better communication? Safety? Great literary quality? Just like anything in life, the end influences the journey, so know what you want out of your SOP before beginning it.

- **A picture is worth...** Don't be afraid to use illustrations, diagrams, or flow charts in your SOP. Sometimes a simple illustration does a better job of explaining something than hundreds of words.

- **It's alive!** Once you have completed the SOP for your business, don't just put it up on a shelf and forget it, pulling it down only to prove to someone how badly they screwed up. Constantly update your manual. Capture new realities and creative solutions, and prune out old dead policies that no longer apply. You know you have something of value when employees refer to it to be more productive and to head off conflict before it comes to you.

Have your Standard Operating Procedure manual present at every major staff meeting, and include a regular review of older items as an item on meeting agendas.

If you are committing to the longer-term project of moving from a basic SOP towards a franchise manual or something of that scale, then your SOP manual will grow. It is important not only to prune it, but to subdivide it appropriately. There is no point in giving a new employee a 200-page document as a training manual. If your SOP starts to approach those dimensions, subdivide it.

Training manuals, job descriptions, departmental manuals, functional manuals (finance, HR, operations, marketing), can all be spun off from the central SOP. We want it to be thorough enough to capture and explain what truly matters most, while not bogging anyone down in the minutiae of your whole operation.

♬

Your written Standard Operating Procedures manual truly is an important document. It is central to achieving a Great Performance in a business. Done right, it is the document of your culture; the culture of your people is the single most important thing in your business. If one of the powerful secrets for a Great Performance is consistency, then your SOP is the script or the score of that consistent performance.

Why would you pour all of your resources into the creation of a Great Performance only to have no way to repeat it consistently, keep it on track, and ultimately get the very most value out of that work when you exit?

A well-written Standard Operating Procedures manual does exactly that. It is the score or script of your Great Performance, nothing less.

♫

Journal Intermission

- What are the most pressing 2 – 3 things you need to improve to make your business more saleable, investable, etc?

- Note one thing you wish you or your employees did more consistently to improve customer experience of your business.

♫♫♫

SCENE 14: Meet Your Coach

Performance Note
"What Got You Here Won't Get You There."
Marshal Goldsmith

Band Camp Performance:

The years go by but everything remains the same. You repeat the same patterns, get into the same problems, rely on the same solutions, and in the end each year looks pretty much like the last. You feel like stuff is constantly coming at you without warning, when the truth is there were many warnings. You just couldn't hear them.

Great Performance:

You pick a direction, and you develop and execute the steps to get you there. You bring in professional coaches and consultants, not because they know better than you, but because they know different from you. You have developed a culture of coaching in your organization, and nasty surprises are the exception, not the rule.

♫

People and relationships have been identified as central throughout this book. Of all the relationships that will facilitate a Great Performance, the most effective is the coaching relationship.

The coaching relationship is critical to designing for maximum value and successful exits. A great coaching relationship is the closest thing a business has to the master classes in the performing arts world. This is the time of the professional observer, the person who has some distance from your reality, yet is able to weave that reality with the dozens or hundreds of other realities the coach has encountered before.

In all fields, the truly successful have coaches and mentors. Whether it is sports, the performing arts, or in business, a culture of success is supported by a culture of coaching.

Let's review what defines a coaching relationship in business and in the rest of life, and why it adds so much value.

Honesty

Consistent, unflinchingly honest feedback about your behaviors and your progress is the heart of the coaching process. This is one of the things that define a coaching relationship (whether with a professional coach, or anyone prepared to play that role in your life or your business). In almost all other relationships, pure honesty is easily compromised by other, often legitimate agendas.

We all know as lovers, spouses, parents, children, employers, employees, and sometimes even as best friends, we pull punches. In our desire to make the other person feel good, or feel supported, we tell them something other than the absolute and sometimes unattractive truth.

The best coaches are those who have no other agenda than your success. They are not your friends, family members, colleagues at work, or anything other than a coach. The truth is their most powerful tool. Where this matters more than anywhere else is in providing feedback on behavior and decisions. In a world where a few words, or a few extra days, can change everything, we need to know from someone who has no agenda, other than our success, whether our behaviors and decisions are supporting or eroding that success.

This addresses the Jim Rohn quote from Act II, *"Failure is not a single, cataclysmic event. You don't fail overnight. Instead, failure is a few errors in judgment, repeated every day."* The only sure protection against that failure is honest feedback about what you are doing, and about what is really going on.

Someone Who's Been There

Coaching is different from mentoring. A mentor more typically tends to be from inside your world, someone who has been there before. This familiarity with your world goes deeper than just understanding your industry, and can include having experience in your actual job within your specific company.

A good coaching relationship does include some degree of mentoring. It is powerful to work with someone who understands your world, whether that is your business, your position, your industry, or your market.

The challenge is to find the right mix of mentorship and coaching. On the behavioural, managerial, or leadership levels, the outsider stance of a coach has great value. The closer you get to looking for support in a specific area, the less valuable a generalist is and the more valuable a coach who can also be a mentor.

Though there are many others, two areas specifically stand out in this regard: sales and manufacturing productivity.

1. Sales coaching requires knowledge of economics, psychology, and of the methodology of great sales technique.
2. Manufacturing consulting requires similarly intimate knowledge of operations, supply chain and inventory management, and systems like ISO or SixSigma.

Typically at those levels of detail, support is best provided by a mentor from the inside, or a specialist consultant from the outside. Knowing what outcomes you seek is important before deciding whether the best resource is a consultant, coach, or mentor.

I am a business coach with a great deal of knowledge about how small businesses work. Small businesses are a unique world where there is a great deal of blurring between things like management, finance, productivity, and marketing. These mixes create situations you simply don't find in the more compartmentalized and specialized world of larger organizations. My rule of thumb is if an organization has more than 2 to 3 divisions, 20 to 30 employees, or annual revenues in excess of 10 million, they typically require a degree of specialized support I do not offer. They need a consultant or access to mentors.

Commitment

The coaching relationship is a formal one with a clear commitment to a particular process. If you have hired a professional coach, the commitment is built in; however, that commitment can be made between friends, colleagues, mentors at work, or other team members.

In this area, there is only one truly key difference between a professional coach and one of the other hybrid (for example, a coworker-coach) roles: you can fire your coach. Sure you can do something similar in the other relationships too, but it gets a lot messier.

Accountability

A coach helps you be accountable for your commitments. A coach helps you monitor your progress and encourages you to complete tasks you have committed to.

Accountability is honesty applied to action. With your coach you commit to a specific vision or outcome, negotiate the steps required to get there, and then make a commitment to execute those steps. You give your coach permission to hold you accountable for your actions.

Outside Perspective

We all have blind spots. The best coaching relationships let the perceptions of another person help us avoid old patterns or existing prejudices. This is where you have to balance working with someone who gets your world, yet still retains some of that outsider perspective. To paraphrase an old saying: if we both see only the same thing, one of us is redundant.

Performance Note
"You must look within for value,
but must look beyond for perspective."
Denis Waitley

One could argue this is the other heart of coaching: the ability to provide a perspective from outside your life or outside the organization. That external perspective has two values:

1. **Ignorance.** Sometimes we're prevented from making creative choices or bold leaps because we know too much. History and past failures cause us to dismiss or avoid taking certain risks even if they might be just the thing to do. Taking an uncalculated risk is dangerous, but not nearly as dangerous as taking no risks at all.
2. **Diversified experience.** A professional coach can bring the combined experiences of every business with whom he or she has worked to achieve similar results in the past. Sometimes the best solutions are lateral ones: perhaps the best way to solve a cash-flow problem in an accounting firm is with a model developed in a landscaping company.

♫

Unconditional Support

Owning a small business is hard on almost every aspect of your life. There are moments where everything feels like it is going backward. In those moments, a coach provides support, encouragement, comfort, and the confidence you need to refocus on your journey. Coaching support is unconditional and without judgment. This is why it is so important for both client and coach to ensure there is a solid fit in the relationship.

There are two important elements to this:

1. I like you. One thing I say to almost every prospective client sometime in our first conversation is: "We need to know if we can stand to be in the same room together." I say this with warmth and humour to send the message I am not deadly serious all the time. This relationship has to be real, human, and sometimes funny. The message is clear nonetheless: we must click socially and emotionally. If that is missing, all the professionalism in the world will not allow me to create the absolute, no-punches-pulled support you need.
2. I'm a cherry picker. My support must be conditional on your ability to pay for it and use it. That is why I conduct a formal assessment and take so much time (up to 3 months) getting to know a client's business, before getting to work on setting goals and making big decisions.

In the financial ups and downs of my clients' businesses, I must believe in the likelihood of their success. In a relationship that can last up to three years, that kind of assurance is important.

♩

Where Can I Find A Coach?

Hire A Professional

A good professional coach should meet every one of the criteria listed above. One challenge can be clarity about whether a consultant, coach, or mentor is best suited to the present moment. A good coach or consultant can help you answer that question. They will always work with you to determine the amount of specific technical or operational knowledge a person in their position must have to be successful.

If they don't see the fit, a good coach will always back out of the assignment gracefully and before too much money is spent.

If formal mentoring is a better fit for your situation, particularly in the area of management, check out the work of Henry Mintzberg, the author of *Managing*, and other books. The home of Mintzberg's fantastic project on managers mentoring each other, is at coachingourselves.com.

Work With A Peer

This is usually more mentoring than coaching, but the distinction is sometimes arbitrary. Following on Mintzberg's work, your best coaches can be your peers: other employees of your organization who are of similar experience and share similar levels of responsibility. It goes without saying the greatest strength of this model is you would be working with people intimate with the nuances of your business and your world.

The challenge is you may collectively not be able to see the forest for the trees.

♫

Where NOT To Go

A Friend

This is just as tricky as any other aspect of working with a friend in business. The kinds of dynamics that make for great friendships are not necessarily the same for a great coaching relationship. If things go wrong, are you prepared to sacrifice a friendship? As I often tell people considering hiring a friend or going into business with them. "You can hire a friend, but can you fire a friend?"

A Direct Report

I don't believe it is possible to transcend the power dynamics in management-and-employee, or junior-partner-and-senior-partner relationships. An unequal power relationship and coaching are incompatible. Sooner or later a junior will pull a punch for fear of repercussions.

Family

See "A friend" above! This one is the hardest of all and I don't recommend it. The stumbling points are not only the probable reluctance to make hard calls, including ending the relationship, but there are also the emotional histories and cultural conditioning that come with most family relationships. The kind of detachment critical to good coaching is pretty much impossible to find here.

♫

The coaching relationship is critical to the Great Performance of a business. The honest feedback on decisions and behaviors, the global perspective, and the support in holding you accountable for the sometimes difficult steps that need to be taken, cannot be found in any other way.

These are the same reasons no great performer or athlete would consider an attempt at greatness without a master or coach. No one gets there alone. Nowhere is this more true than in the areas covered here in Act III: shifting your focus from working in the business to managing others to work in the business, and developing a long-term strategy to maximize the value of your business with an eye to getting the most out of it you possibly can.

Building that team and building that value are necessary but challenging. Checking your decisions with professionals like accountants, lawyers, and coaches can ensure you achieve your dreams without too much time and money wasted on blind alleys.

♬

Journal Intermission

- Write down some areas you are unsure or uncertain about in the long-term growth of your business.

- What is one task you know is important for the long-term success of your business, but that you tend to avoid?

- If there is one area of your leadership or management style you would like to improve, what would it be?

♫♫♫

SCENE 15: The Owner Takes A Bow

Performance Note

"If you want a happy ending,
that depends, of course, on where you stop your story."

Orson Wells

I wrote at the start of this chapter from the moment your business is up and on its legs, you must start finding ways to maximize its value beyond your monthly owner's draws.

This will help you grow a business that is so fine tuned, the script or score so well-written, and everyone so well rehearsed in their roles that when you decide to move on, and how, is almost irrelevant. Everything is always in a state of readiness for this moment. Whether you walk out the door on Friday to return after two weeks' holiday, bring in new partners, or leave never to return again, having sold the business at a huge gain to you, doesn't matter. The business is always ready because it is always at its best.

There are two values in every business Great Performance: the earnings it generates for its owners, and the latent value it holds as a beautifully managed asset.

This final scene is about maximizing both of those values.

♫

Your Primary Focus

Here is the rule that guarantees Great Performances in this area:

You must constantly move out of your business. *You must move towards greater leadership responsibilities, and increasingly focus on Deep Cycle work.* You must find a way to have others focus on the day-to-day and even month-to-month operations of your business. Your responsibility is increasingly to lead the whole enterprise into the future.

If you are the owner and you are spending more than an hour or two, or 30% of your days, on the shop floor, a primary goal must be to continue to grow your team.

If you are an independent professional who measures billable hours (consultant, stylist, coach, physiotherapist, lawyer) this still applies to you. Clearly your billable hours are the foundation of your business, particularly at the beginning, but there will come a time when you hit a ceiling: when you are working as many hours as you can, your waiting list is full, and you are charging the maximum you can in your market.

You still need to find a way to move out of the focus on the Current Cycle of your business or you will be at that level for the rest of your career.

This would mean in the present, things like growing your business, taking sick days, or taking longer holidays will all remain a challenge, and at the end of your run, when it comes time to exit, you will have nothing to sell.

♫

Writing The Ending

Many authors and composers will tell you one of the most challenging parts of their process is finding a good ending. Any business and almost any process within a business have the same challenge.

For every Casablanca-quality ending there are thousands of, *"Dark and stormy night…"* beginnings (and ironically, how the ending of Casablanca was arrived at is a story in itself!). How many of us have begun something only never to finish it, from exercise commitments and diets, to music lessons or the next great American novel?

In the performing arts, the ending isn't everything, but it is extremely important. How a film, dance, or a musical composition ends gives the whole thing a feeling of making sense. Not always on a literal sense, but on a deeper aesthetic sense. It just feels right, even if the ending is surprising or illogical on a rational or surface level.

In business, the ending matters just as much. It makes everything you have done over the last 5 or 10 or 43 years make sense if the story ends well. It helps you answer that question I began Act III with, and that friends and family often ask, *"Why are you in business?"*

So how does all that happen?

Start At The Beginning

Performance Note
A standing ovation is seldom a surprise.

At the top of Act III we looked at important elements of the process of working yourself out of the picture. Delegating, committing to your priorities, developing and documenting systems, and creating a leadership supported by coaching are all critical to making this transition successfully.

One thing you cannot do is start all that only near the end. You cannot because the end seldom comes when you expect it. Even if it did, no business can be properly prepared for an exit, sale, franchising, or any other form of realizing its value as an asset, in less than 3 years. Unplanned exits are seldom pretty. Even if a competitor or larger player buys you out, if your priorities, systems, and team are not at the very best, you will not get the price you want. Though in the tough world of business, you may get the price you deserve.

I will say it one more time: from the moment your business baby is up and teetering along on its first steps, start to plan for graduation. Look to the future, and begin to implement the Deep

Cycle processes that will help you write that memorable ending.

It is also worth repeating that great long-term planning is not only valuable in preparing your exit, it also leads to a Great Performance before you take that final bow. The best way to get a standing ovation at the end is to design a Great Performance from the beginning.

It's All In The Timing

One of the jobs you have in the Deep Cycle is to keep your weather eye on the future. This is where a great coaching relationship can help you. In conversation and reflection, things that might be niggling at you in the back of your mind can reveal early warning signs of impending change.

Staying on top of your industry, the news, and social media is also important in developing a great sense of timing. A business leader in pursuit of a lifelong Great Performance cannot read too much, listen too much, converse too much (that's conversing; not talking), or take too much time soaking up the signals of the world around them. A leader cannot spend too much time exploring future possibilities with her team.

Do everything you can to be the fortune teller your team needs you to be. This is because your business and the market may dictate that it is time to franchise, invest, expand, or sell before you are personally or operationally ready for that to happen.

Work to be ready every day.

♫

A business, like many perishable commodities, has a peak price. This is determined by both internal and external factors. You want to sell when your profits are strong, your revenues growing (typically steady growth for at least 3 consecutive years), your labour turnover minimal, any equipment or buildings working and looking their best, foreseeable demand for your products or services is strong, and no major industry-changing threats lie on the horizon.

When, through conversations with your advisors and through your own readings of the currents around you, you get the signal it is time to act, you have two choices:

1. You can jump/sell/split at that peak moment; or...
2. You postpone and reinvest in another cycle, bring the business to even greater heights, and consider your options at another time in the future.

The advantage of the first choice is you have much less risk. Reinvesting in another growth cycle might make you more money in the future, or the market could go completely sideways.

One thing you should be aware of if you sell with plans to start another business: if you do sell, there will almost certainly be a non-competition clause in the purchase agreement. This will prevent you from starting up a similar business in the same market. If the business you are selling is the only thing you are good at doing in the whole world, you will have to move to a different territory (the non-competition agreement could make that another continent), or you might want to consider option 2.

Can The Band Play On Without You?

Performance Note
The value of your business should be measured by how long it could continue without you.

Many purchasers will look for a competent management team to be in place. Here we are again: surrounding yourself with good people is everything, even in a business you are leaving!

217

A great management team not only supports you by freeing you to grow the business to this point, but it also reassures the new owners the business will thrive after you have booked your tickets for Miami.

Kevin O'Leary, one of the investor stars of the Canadian business reality program *The Dragons' Den*, calls this the *"hit by a bus"* factor. If you get hit by a bus tomorrow, what happens to your business? If it can't go on without you, it is worthless to an investor. It is a warning sign you don't have a Great Performance on your hands yet. The only business worth buying, by definition, is one that will continue to run when you no longer own it.

The new owners can always install a management team of their own, but that proposition is fraught with problems, almost always causes problems with the employees who remain behind, and generally eats away at productivity, customer service, and profit, while the new team gets up to speed. Having a great management team in place, along with the SOP described above, ensures continuity. *Continuity* is one of the biggest value points when it is there, and a deal breaker when it is absent.

The Money's Different Here

The area of business finances is one of the few where the exit practices differ from the performance practices.

A business in mid-growth cycle often seeks to minimize taxes, invests in long-term growth (and consequently is tolerant of some level of long-term debt), finds specific synergies in the combinations of various activities, assets, and liabilities.

On the other hand, a business ready to sell needs to look very closely at its debt and equity levels, major assets like real estate (which is often sold separately), and how it reports revenues and expenses.

What might be good business when it comes to reporting to the tax man, may not be good business when it comes to reporting to a buyer or investor. In this area, perhaps more than any other, it is important to consult a specialist, in this case an accountant with a track record in preparing businesses for sale.

The other area where a specialist is as critical is in drawing up the actual contract for purchase and sale, or the investment of new partners. This is not the time to use a template from the internet, or even just any lawyer. This could be the sale of a lifetime we are talking about here - literally. The only person you should even consider handling this for you is a lawyer specializing in business and contract law.

The Great Wine Factor

Just for a moment, let's leave the area of the performing arts to turn to another one of my favourite worlds: that of wine.

Great wines are mature and complex; we want your customers to be exactly the same. Not individually of course, but as a collective group, they have to be complex in the sense they require more than just one thing from you, and mature in that they didn't just show up on your doorstep last month.

Once again, this is as important for a Great Performance in your business right now, as it will be for the grand finale.

The Mature Buyer

Prospective business buyers and investors do not look for single instances of good news, they look for trends. They need to see that your customers have stuck with you over time.

One of my rules is rates of acquisition and defection tend to mirror each other. That means if you acquired a thousand customers overnight, that's about how quickly most of them will leave. Sticky, long-term relationships take time to build, as we learned in Act I.

Buyers and investors want to see not only that you have a mature, stable customer base, but that it shows clear signs of continued growth.

It's All About Layers

Buyers and investors need to know if one product, line, SKU, design, or service goes out of favour with the market, that your business can continue based on other flavours.

No one wants to buy a business or drink a wine that is all over the place, lacking character and focus. At the same time, a complete lack of interest, complexity, or variety makes for a boring wine and a high-risk business.

A one-trick-pony is not only boring, it can be a poor business investment.

No Actor's Nightmare Please

There is a great theatre improvisation game called *Actor's Nightmare*. In it, a pair of actors improvise a scene on stage. One of the actors has a script; the other one doesn't. The script is selected at random by someone other than the two actors. The actor with the script begins to read lines, and the actor without the script must improvise responses. Between the two of them they must create a scene that makes sense.

The game is a favourite amongst improv instructors because only half the dialogue must be made up, so beginning improvisers find the structure less intimidating. They don't have to make up the whole thing. *Actor's Nightmare* is based on a common—and real—nightmare many actors have. In it, they walk on stage and everyone seems to know what is going on except them. If you've ever had that nightmare you'll know what a terrifying feeling it is.

The business equivalent to the actor's nightmare is buying a business that has no documented policies or procedures.

I introduced the solution in Scene 13: Standard Operating Procedures (SOP). I am bringing them up here again because of how important they are. Not only are SOPs mandatory for a Great Performance while you own your business, they are perhaps even more important when you sell it or seek other forms of investment or expansion. While you were the sole owner of your business, you could at least manage a *Band Camp performance* without documented procedures because for the most part you have everything in your head. New owners or partners will not be so lucky.

A Franchise Of One

The rule for a Great Performance is simple: always run your business so if you closed up shop on Friday afternoon, a new owner could come in Monday and, without any transition, turn on the lights, pick up your Standard Operating Procedures manual, and get back to the business of making money.

To follow on our discussion of franchises and franchise manuals earlier, another way to think of this is you should run your business like a franchise even if it isn't one. All the planning, organizing, documenting, and focus on consistency, consistency, consistency that a great franchise builds is exactly what you should be building on.

You are a franchise of one.

♫

The Nuances Of The Score

A business can be sold as an asset sale or a share sale. This means you must decide whether you are selling the company and its shares (assuming it is an incorporated business) or just the assets it owns (buildings, equipment, etc.).

That decision is one of the most important ones in the whole process. It has huge implications on the amount of the sale, on the taxes you will pay (or won't pay) on that sale, and what kinds of buyers will even consider the purchase.

The process is further complicated by the country in which you are reading this book. In each country, there are different incorporations available to you, and different rules around the disposal of shares or assets.

The legal and financial complexities of this are considerable and beyond the scope of this book, but to ensure you do get that standing ovation to your Great Performance, there are two things you must consider:

1. **Structure.** If you know right from the outset you will sell the business you are starting in less than ten years, work very closely with a good accountant and an experienced business lawyer (and only a business or corporate lawyer) to *structure* your business in a way that it is optimized for sale.
2. **Restructure.** If you have already owned the business for many years, but know now you will be selling within the next 10 years, again consult specialized accounting and legal professionals to review, and potentially *restructure* your business to optimize it for sale.

This is so important because critically important pieces like the decision to dispose of real-estate assets or to alter the share structure of your business must be done right, and timing is critical. Making changes like this too soon or too late could have huge impacts on the value of your business to a buyer, and to the taxes you may have to pay on the sale.

♫

Exit, Stage Right

Performance Note
*Activities in the next phase of your life
must be more than recreational,
they must be meaningful*

With all the planning for the sale of the business, do not forget the most important piece of the picture, particularly if you are selling to retire: your own life.

When you have owned a business for the better part of your life, it can be the thing you identify with more than anything else. That business is you. Prepare for your exit by preparing yourself. Like so much in business and in life, if you don't plan your exit, you can't complain when the unplanned happens. If you don't plan for the transition, the day you don't show up for work will feel like the emptiest day in your life. Depression and related illnesses are not uncommon when that transition does not go well.

You will tire of holidays, you may tire of golf or gardening. No matter how compelling a retirement brochure may make these kinds of activities look, trust me, they are no substitutes for life in the small-business trenches. You must fill the new space in your life with something more than recreational; it must be meaningful.

Above all, consider activities that add value to your life and the lives of others. Part-time work, volunteer work, turning a hobby into a small business (this time without the pressure for it to be successful), are all options I have seen work well.

Just don't plan to do nothing.

Manage Your Debt For The Exit

Don't just focus on the revenue from the sale of your business. They won't go far if too much of it goes into paying overloaded credit-card debt each month. Making that exit debt-free has as much positive impact on your quality of life as the dollars you earn from the sale of your business.

You Are Still The Star Of Your Own Life

Don't just focus on business, especially in those last 10 years before you exit. You will not be able to take advantage of your new freedoms and opportunities if you are not healthy and fit. Whether you retire fully, work part time, or start something completely new, your enjoyment of any activity will be heavily impacted by your health.

What I have said before is still true here: what is good for your exit is good for you and your business now too. Your physical and financial health, a positive forward-looking vision, healthy routines and habits, will all help you inspire a great standing ovation in the end, but they also ensure a Great Performance for all the years you are still in the business.

♪

Journal Intermission

- Take a moment and visualize your final exit from your business. What will it look like? Will you stay to manage? Will you sell completely? Will you franchise or hand it over to your kids? When will it happen? What value will it provide for you? How will you feel on the last day in the role you have now? Write a paragraph or two as if this were the ending of a story. A great story.

- List 3 things you could start tomorrow in your business that would help you ensure the conclusion of your Great Performance is a standing ovation.

♫♫♫

Summary

You began your business with a dream.

End it with a standing ovation: turn and face your family, your friends, your employees, and your customers (if you have done it right, many of those people will be in more than one category), and take a bow. Take a bow knowing you deserve every good thing you have made, and all the recognition you are receiving now. To get to that standing ovation is an incredibly difficult journey. If you began things right, and built your business on the principles outlined in this book, you have a very good chance of getting there.

Keeping the dream alive is not some abstract slogan here. It is what you are really doing when you insist on doing things right consistently and with passion day after day. That is how you keep the dream you had for your business alive and thriving for all the years that you own it.

Most business owners didn't include that great standing ovation at the end as part of their dream when they started their business. They wanted independence, and an opportunity to do things on their own terms. They probably hoped for a possibility of greater returns on their labours than they would have received as employees. But most small-business owners don't think much past that. Independence, food on the table, the kids through college; that's about as far as the dream goes. It is the job of this book, and particularly of Act III, to lift your dream higher.

For a truly Great Performance, you can't just see the beginning and the middle; you have to be able to write the ending. No great story, no great play or piece of music, is complete without that great ending. A business without a great ending for its owner is more than just a work not completed. It is a tragedy, as the Band Camp performance at the start of Act III reminds us.

To achieve that transformative ending you need to put a few things into place:

- A team to help you, including people specifically there to coach and mentor you.
- A process to move from working in the Current Cycle of your business to working on the planning and vision of the Deep Cycle.
- A commitment to creating a written document of how your business works, and a plan of how you will exit.

Don't wait until you are thinking every day about getting out. Begin at the beginning. Start thinking and planning about your exit the day you start your business. Or at the very least, start now. This is my parting word to you: *begin as you would have things end.*

A business cannot help but be a Great Performance if the ending is considered from the moment it is begun, and is run every day as if that end would come tomorrow. The care, the passion, the long vision...all come together when a performance is approached this way.

That's it. You're on. Break a leg.

♬♬♬

Master Class: Maximizing Value

Check the boxes as you go through this. These points are not optional. There is no great performance until you have checked off 100% of the boxes!

The *Do This Now* items are marked to indicate that if you do not have these in place in your business, forget the list, and do these now!

The day-to-day execution of these items would take another book to describe. That might be coming. In the meantime, hire a good business coach to guide you through these steps.

☐
1. **Do a review of your typical week.** Determine how much time you are committing to Current, Growth, and Deep Cycle work (review Act II if you need to refresh your memories as to what kinds of activities these are). If you are in the mature phase of your business, you should be spending less than 30% of your time on Current Cycle work.

_____
_____
_____

☐
2. **Make a list of all the ways your business could possibly make money** while you away on holiday. Be creative.

_____
_____
_____

☐

3. **State clearly the ONE thing you do best** in your business. Only one.

_____

_____

_____

☐

4. **Calculate what that activity is worth to your business.**

_____

_____

_____

☐

5. **Make a list of EVERYTHING in your business** someone else could do.

_____

_____

_____

☐

6. **Make a passive income plan.** Work with your business coach and team to determine how many of the ideas from #5 are feasible, and how and when they can be implemented

_____

_____

_____

☐

7. **Create a Replacing Myself schedule** that sets out a vision for when each of these activities will be taken over by someone else.

_____

_____

_____

☐

8. **Create a list of all the hiring, co-op, internships, mentoring, other para-employment programs** and wage-subsidy programs that your community offers.

_____

_____

_____

☐

9. **Determine your growth-critical position.** Which one position, if you could hire for it next, would make the biggest difference to your growth?

_____

_____

_____

☐

10. Pricing to leverage growth. Review your pricing structures. Determine how much you would have to raise your prices without increasing revenues to afford that position.

_____

_____

_____

☐

11. Meet with your coach, accountant, or other advisors to review your options for changing your business model to make expanding your team or increasing your passive income possible.

_____

_____

_____

☐

12. Create a Leadership Calendar. What would your calendar look like if you were only doing what you did best in your business? The object is to create a vision with dates.

_____

_____

_____

☐

13. What does your attention cycle look like? What is the ideal work cycle for you? 20 minutes? 4 hours? For how long can you be maximally productive? This should be reflected in your leadership calendar above.

_____

_____

_____

☐

14. Have a Leadership Calendar meeting with your team. Discuss what the implications of your ideal calendar are. Who will do what is not on that calendar but still needs to get done? What would you have to do as a team to make this real?

_____

_____

_____

☐

15. Create and document routines. Meet with your team and work to create routines out of everything that can be made routine. Write the routines down as part of your Standard Operating Procedures (SOP).

_____

_____

_____

☐

16. Write out your mission statement. *Do This Now* If you don't have a mission statement, create one. If you have one, print out a copy as the first page of your SOP.

_____

_____

_____

☐

17. List all your roles. Identify each role in your organization, and write a brief one-page description of what they do. Better yet, have the person in the role write the description!

_____

_____

_____

☐

18. Issue note books. Purchase an inexpensive notebook for each employee (do you have a Dollar Store in your area?). Ask employees to track ideas and mistakes in the notebooks and bring them to staff meetings.

_____

_____

_____

☐

19. Describe your customer experience cycle. For your Standard Operating Procedures manual, write out everything you do to promote to, complete a transaction with, and follow up with your customers.

_____

_____

_____

☐

20. Describe your current cycle. For your SOP, describe everything your business does to deliver its services or products, or to manufacture its products.

_____

_____

_____

☐

21. Professional due diligence. As sections that deal with employee performance or expectations are written into your SOP, have them reviewed by a HR professional to ensure compliance with local labor regulations.

_____

_____

_____

☐

22. Hire a business coach. No Great Performance is possible without professional mentors and coaches. Get one on your side.

_____

_____

_____

☐

23. Exit options. With your coach and your team, review your options for what you will do with your business when you are ready to exit.

_____

_____

_____

☐

24. Consider your options. Take time to develop a post-ownership vision and plan. Consider working with a professional like a retirement coach or a business exit strategist to educate yourself about the options.

_____

_____

_____

♫♫♫

More Great Performance Guides

Writers, books, and blogs that have made a difference in my own performances.

People, Marketing, Management

David Rendall - The Freak Factor
(www.drendall.com)
The book that takes the concept of "unique is valuable" and pushes it back in your face by asking if being truly unique rests more in your supposed weaknesses than your strengths, are you prepared to embrace and celebrate those weaknesses? A great blog on getting to a Great Performance by owning your inner freak.

John Jantsch - The Referral Engine
If there is one name I associate with marketing for small business, it is John Jantsch and the Duct Tape Marketing blog. I read it religiously, and it has informed much of my thinking about effective marketing for small business. I'll put it as plainly as I can: if you aren't reading this blog, or using Jantsch's various marketing guides and kits, your marketing isn't everything it could be. Jantsch's book The Referral Engine is probably the best book written on word-of-mouth marketing.

Steve Yastrow - We
It's simple: pretty much everything I write about customer experience and the primacy of relationships in business originates from this book. It connected instantly the first time I read it. This is a must-read for any business owner. You can read my review of We here: www.smbfundamentals.com/book-review/we-by-steve-yastrow-2

Bret L. Simmons - P.O.B. Positive Organizational Behavior
(www.bretlsimmons.com)

This is one of my favourite blogs. Bret's writing on management, leadership, and organizational behaviour is always real, immediately useful, and deeply felt. I also love his direct style that swings between raw and challenging. I truly believe that if a business owner read Bret's articles and took his wisdom to heart, the result would be happier and more productive employees, and an organization that people would kill to work for and do business with. It's that good.

Time, Statistics, Numbers, Money

Malcolm Gladwell – Outliers

The book that introduced the 10,000-hour rule to the world. This book, coupled with Leonard Mlodinow's (see below) is foundational to much of what I believe about success and how to have it. In a Twitter-length summary it would be: Luck and talent matter, but nothing matters more than experience and persistence.

Leonard Mlodinow – The Drunkard's Walk

After a rich and fascinating journey through the history and mathematics of probability, one message comes through loud and clear in this book: good luck is mostly the consequence of persistence. The best way to turn up your lucky number is to keep rolling the dice. Many books have influenced my thinking, but if I had to pick one that cemented my faith in clarity, focus, persistence, and hard work in the face of all the voodoo out there in the business self-help bookshelves across the nation, this is it.

David Chilton – The Wealthy Barber
The classic text about managing and growing your personal finances. Very easy to read and full of powerful action items that have transformed lives.

Adam Baker – Man vs Debt
(manvsdebt.com)
A heartfelt and powerful blog that gives both the dream and the tools of living a debt-free life equal time. The subtitle says it all: Sell Your Crap. Live Debt Free. Do What You Love.

John Jantsch – The Logistics of Time
(ducttapemarketing.com/blog/2010/11/19/the-logistics-of-time) This article both inspired my thinking around the 3 Cycles in business, and is itself an excellent approach to bringing a sense of structure and commitment to the complex world of sales.

Daniel Pink – A Whole New Mind
Today, it is pretty much impossible to discuss Deep Cycle planning without including a mention of Pink's book. We often wonder how to go about doing anything that resembles meaningful 'planning' over longer time cycles. This book creates a very thoughtful framework to allow us to think about where we may all be headed, and the role that creativity and empathy will play in that future. Make no decisions about the long term future without reading this book.

Planning, Growth, Management, Exits

Michael E. Gerber – The E-Myth Revisited
While there are areas of this book I disagree with, the central premise is absolutely sound: being a great carpenter does not mean that you will create a great carpentry business. Or as Gerber's website puts it, the E-myth is the Entrepreneurial Myth:

"...the fatal assumption that an individual who understands the technical work of a business can successfully run [that] business." Worth a read if you are ready to think about the whole of owning a business, from beginning to end.

Marcus Buckingham – The One Thing You Need To Know
This fantastic, must-read book covers three areas that have a huge impact on your success in business: leadership, management, and personal success. I owe much of my thinking around management, building great teams, and the roles of focus and emphasizing your strengths in personal success, to the writings of Buckingham.

Marshall Goldsmith – What Got You Here Won't Get You There
If you have read the section on the value of coaching in this book, but still aren't sure, get Goldsmith's book. In it, Goldsmith not only lays out the behaviours that derail great leadership and management, but also details their impact on the careers of his clients, some of the most powerful CEO's and leaders in the world. Read this book and learn how coaching can transform lives, the power of a team-based approach, and the consequences of ignoring behaviour as a key factor in great leadership.

Anthony Bourdain – Kitchen Confidential (and other books)
Not a business book, but still a hugely influential book in my life. When I read this I found probably the best text I had read yet on the art, craft, and business of living a great life. Bourdain drives home in chapter after chapter and book after book the truth that a great experience is forged both out of creative passion and a religious attention to detail and consistency.

Henry Mintzberg - Managing

I think it is enough to say that if you want to read one book on the actual nuts and bolts of what it takes to become a remarkable manager, Mintzberg's book is your ticket. The work is based on Mintzbergs observations of 29 different managers in environments as different as refugee camps and symphony orchestras. Want to manage better? Just read Managing and act on what you learn

Author Biography

 Clemens Rettich speaks a new business language that combines the vocabulary of business with the discipline and creativity of the performing arts. Clemens' strengths as a business coach lie in his layers of education and experience in business, education, and the arts.

Clemens believes passionately in the power of combing an ambitious vision with a commitment to the details. After years as a business owner, a manager, and a team leader, he knows that successfully building a small business is more craft and art than science. Supporting small business clients from almost every industry, and of almost every size, from 100,000 to over 10 million in revenues. He is a mentor, speaker, and contract instructor at the Peter B. Gustavson School of Business at the University of Victoria. He sits on community boards and supports community economic development as a facilitator and consultant. He is a volunteer with Junior Achievement Canada, educating high school students in the fundamentals of business and career development.

We're Not Done Yet...

Great Performances may be the consequence of a lot of hard work, but this book on Great Performances is just the beginning. How would you like to work through the concepts and great practices introduced in this book and work with your own coach and incorporate them into your business?

I can help you do that.

One way is through a one-on-one coaching process with me. I work with businesses anywhere in the world to identify the possibilities and the gaps, and address them systematically and successfully to propel real growth. We use Skype and other online group work tools. When you are ready to grow your business into what it could be next, send me a note at **clemens@clemensrettich.com**.

Greatperformances.ca

The Practice Continues

Or join me online. If you would prefer to work through the various ideas and strategies of Great Performances in a cost-effective and highly flexible environment, join me online at www.greatperformances.ca. Here you will find a gateway to my online coaching programs that cover every topic in this book. There are dozens of programs that guide you step by step in incorporating Great Performance techniques into your business. And I walk with you through it every step of the way.

Greatperformances.ca is not just a glorified eBook or automated website. It is an online coaching environment where I personally work with you, guiding your learning and supporting the execution of each step in your business.

The topics covered in the online coaching program I have designed for readers of Great Performances include:

- Maximizing the lifetime value of a customer
- Creating the perfect customer experience
- Follow-through to turns fans into brand evangelists
- The heart of effective social marketing
- Building the team for a Great Performance
- Recruiting and Training
- Great management's secret weapon: positive feedback
- Every drop: maximizing scarce resources
- Forget time management: manage your priorities
- How money really works for a business
- The big picture: plans, transitions, and exits.
- The ultimate goal: from self-employed to business-owner
- Writing your own Great Performance: the SOP Manual
- Your power team: fans, gurus, and coaches
- Cashing out: how to get that standing ovation

To find out more, either go to **www.greatperformances.ca** or write to me at **clemens@clemensrettich.com**

If you want to get on the path to be a published author by **Influence Publishing** please go to **www.InspireABook.com**

Inspiring books that influence change

More information on our other titles and how to submit your own proposal can be found at **www.InfluencePublishing.com**

CPSIA information can be obtained at www.ICGtesting.com
Printed in the USA
LVOW060056070613

337366LV00005B/16/P